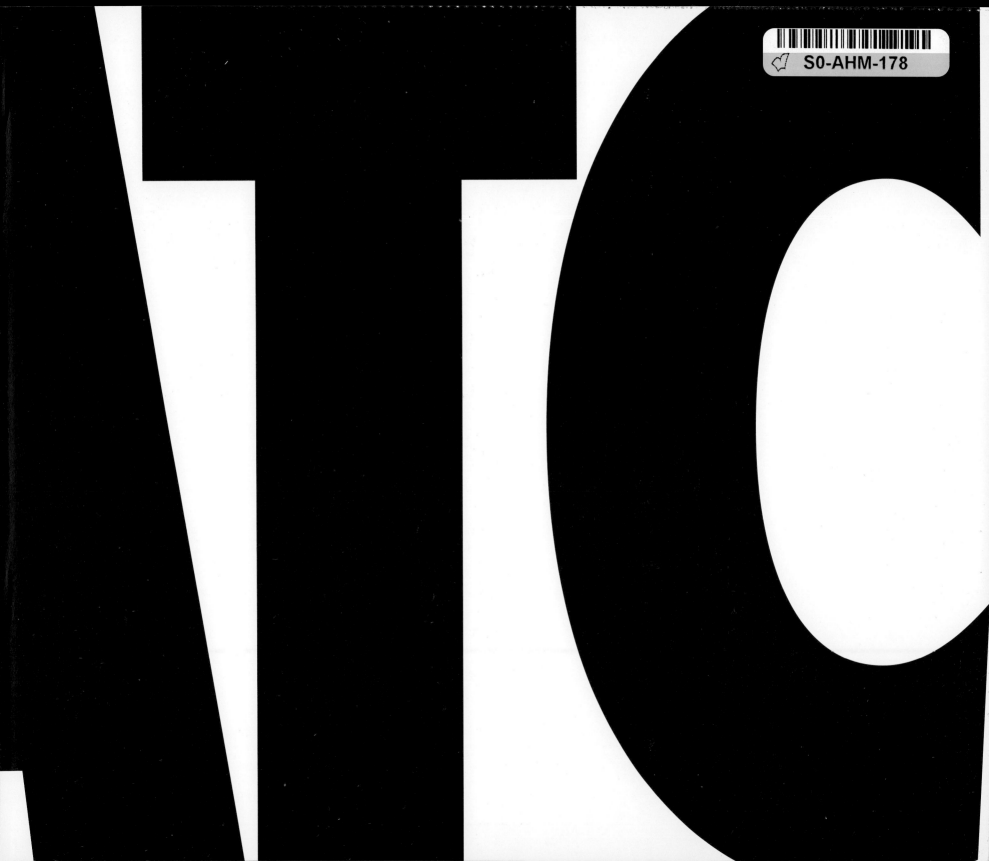

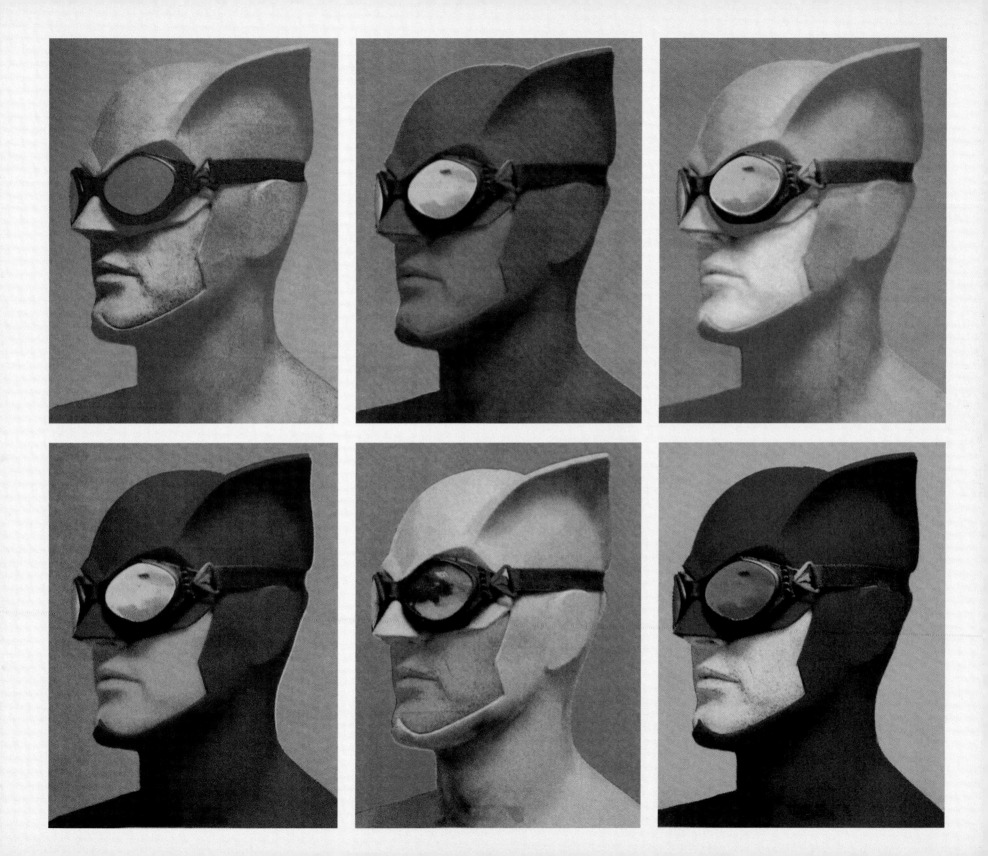

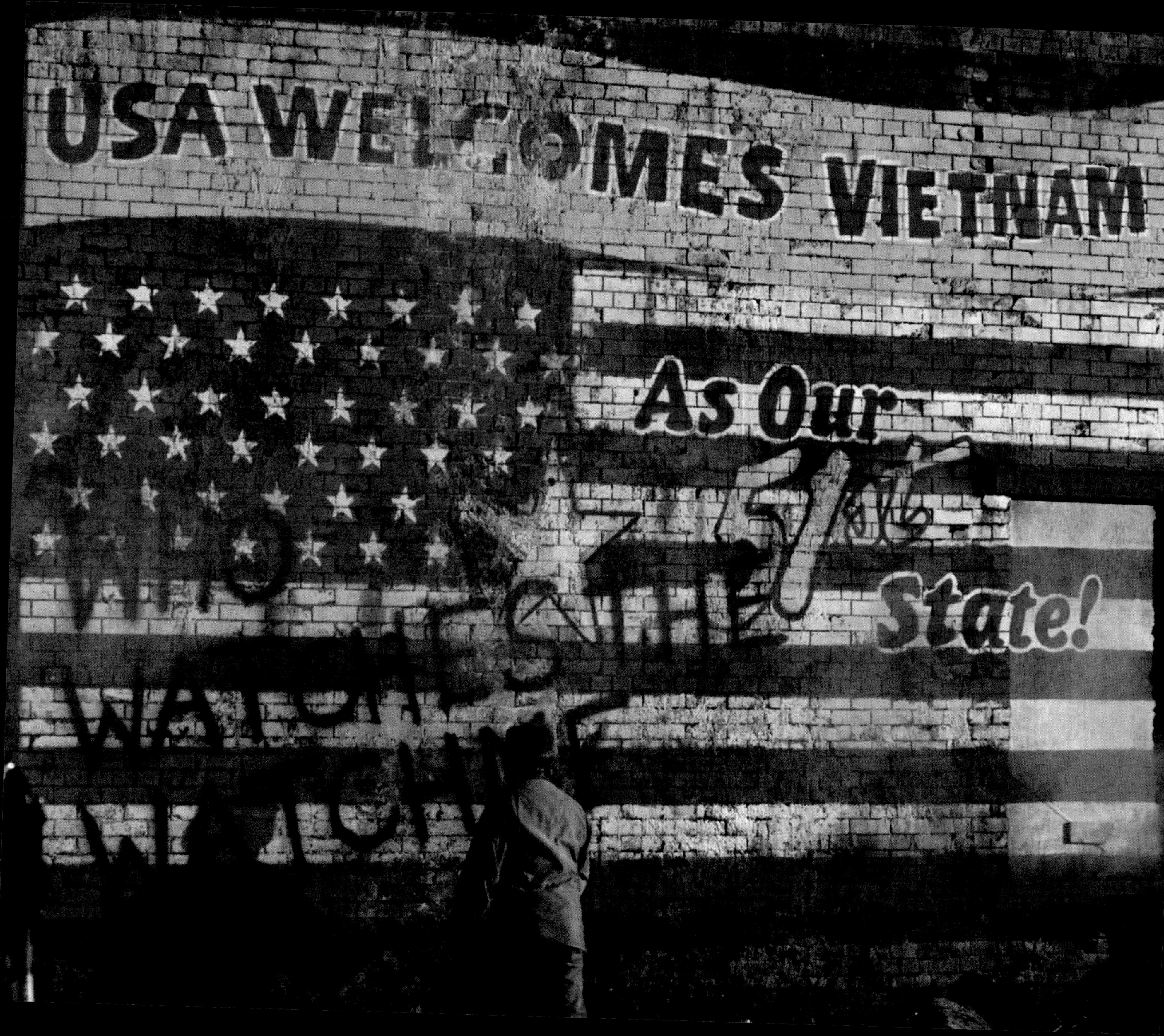
USA WELCOMES VIETNAM
As Our
State!
WHO
THE

CHEMISTRY LABORATORY

←———————————

INTRINSIC FIELD CENTER

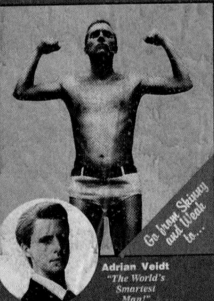

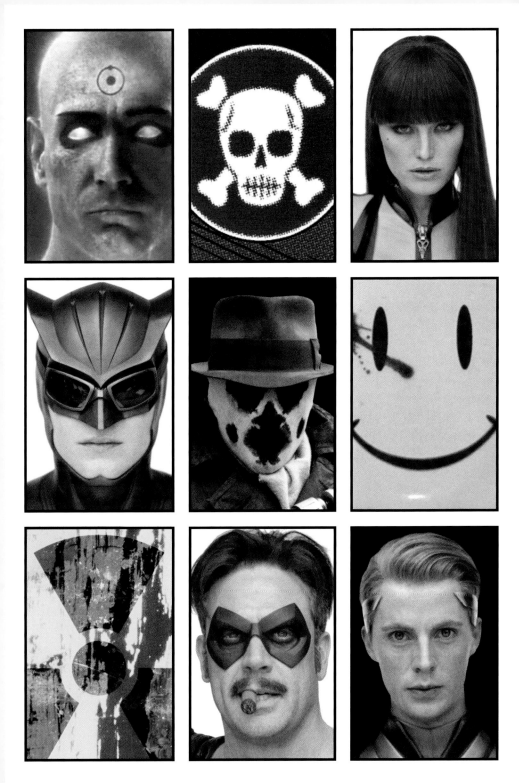

WATC

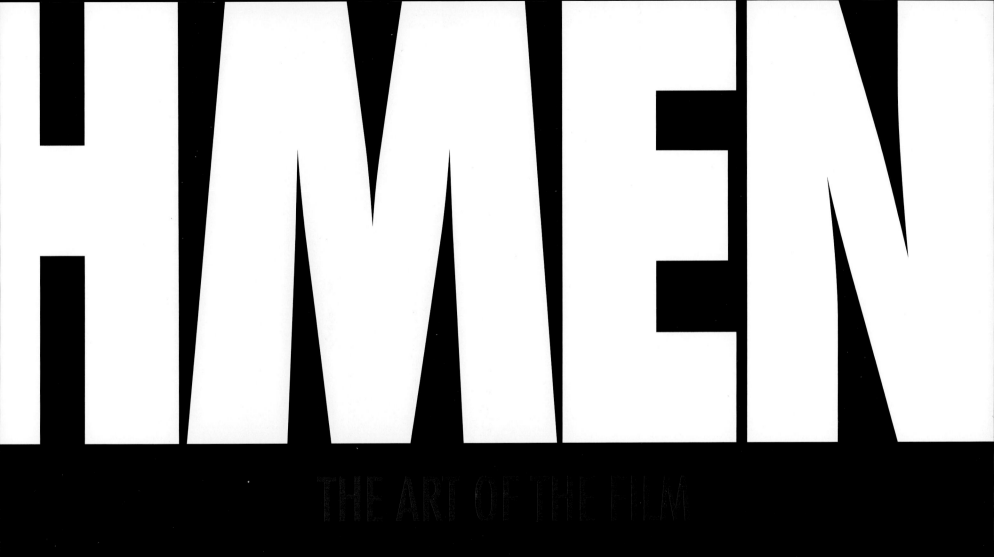

HMEN

THE ART OF THE FILM

PETER APERLO

WATCHMEN THE ART OF THE FILM
9781848560680

Published by Titan Books
A division of Titan Publishing Group Ltd, 144 Southwark St, London SE1 0UP

First edition January 2009
10 9 8 7 6 5 4 3 2

Movie photography by Clay Enos. Photos of Dave Gibbons' archive materials by Dan Scudamore.

Visit our website: **WWW.TITANBOOKS.COM**
Did you enjoy this book? We love to hear from our readers.
Please e-mail us at: **readerfeedback@titanemail.com** or write to Reader Feedback at the above address.

A CIP catalogue record for this title is available from the British Library.

Printed in the USA.

CONTENTS

Little needs to be said about the tremendous influence the deconstructionist graphic novel *Watchmen* has had on the world of super-hero comic books, probably least of all to someone holding this volume. Since the series first began in 1986, comics have become conspicuously darker, grittier, more socially conscious, and above all, more realistic. As much time is now spent exploring super heroes' human foibles (be they physical, psychological, moral, or sexual) as their extraordinary powers, and the vagaries of their complicated personal lives compete for space on the page with their battles against diabolical villains. Super heroes are now more fully anchored in the events of their worlds, and are expected to take responsibility for their actions like never before. For better or worse, they have been forced to grow up.

The reader might also be aware that the impact of *Watchmen* has transcended traditional boundaries, breaking through to the rarified air of the world of literature. On top of winning the comics industry's 1987 Jack Kirby Award for Best Writer/Artist Combination, *Watchmen* has garnered laurels as yet only dreamed of by other graphic novels, including a Hugo Award in 1988 (under the special category "Other Forms") and an honored place on Time Magazine's 2005 list of "100 Best English-Language Novels From 1923 To The Present." The weight of this supreme praise has not been lost on director Zack Snyder. "The cool thing about *Watchmen*," Snyder says, "was that it was instantly viewed as a classic, as a work of literature that was beyond its own genre."

Perhaps the main reason for this mountain of critical acclaim for *Watchmen* is the meticulous marriage of prose and art achieved by writer Alan Moore and artist Dave Gibbons. The artwork in virtually every panel is as richly detailed and multilayered as the plot, the dialogue, and the characters. This is not a book you absorb in one read, or even two. Even after several revisits, some small image or symbol – whether it is a half-glimpsed splash of graffiti, an almost-hidden pyramid, or a subtly formed smiley face – will leap off the page to imbue the scene with that much greater depth of meaning.

The artwork conjures up an America of an alternate 1985 in a way words alone could not. It takes us into a world that is at the same time familiar and unsettlingly alien, but always very, very real. Everywhere are the artifacts of this society – the detritus of its near-apocalyptic pop culture – peeking out at us from the corners of every frame. Gibbons and colorist John Higgins accentuated this unique world by eschewing several conventions common to comic books of the time. There are, for example, no motion lines to denote action, and no onomatopoeic sound effects. Most noteworthy, however, is the conscious avoidance of the primary color palette, which was so prevalent in Golden Age comics. Instead of bright blues and reds, we encounter more often a landscape full of purples, greens, yellows, pinks, browns, and oranges. (The obvious exception is Dr. Manhattan, the only hero with real superpowers, whose cerulean hue clearly marks him as being disconnected from the rest of society.)

"A MASTERPIECE." – TIME MAGAZINE

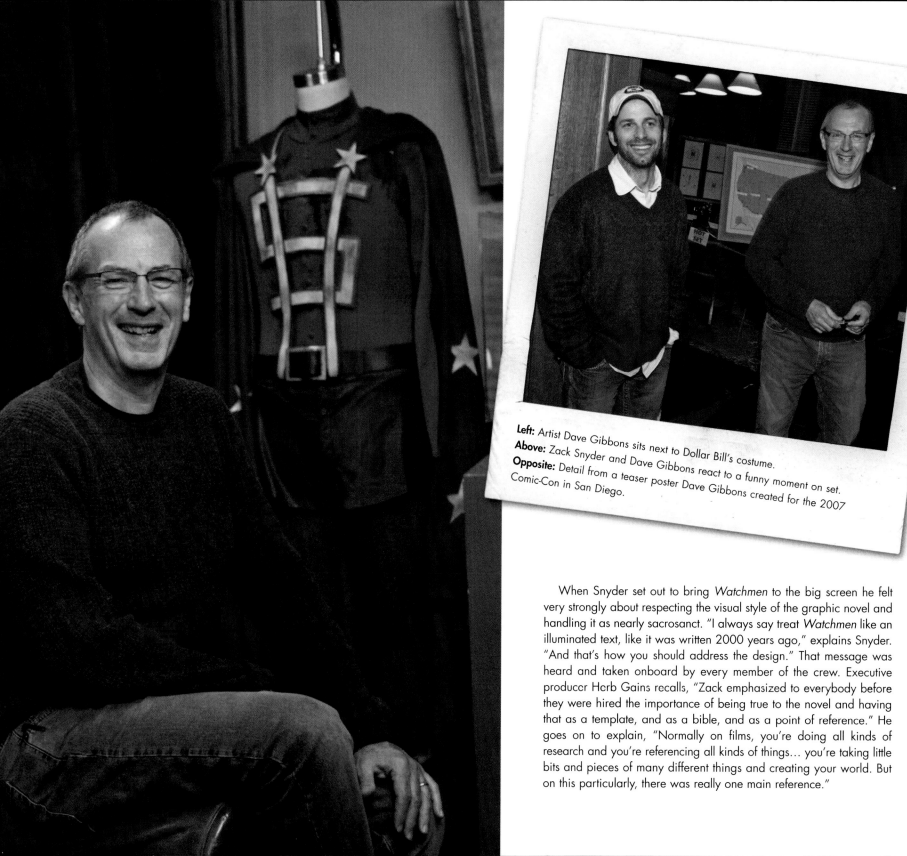

Left: Artist Dave Gibbons sits next to Dollar Bill's costume.
Above: Zack Snyder and Dave Gibbons react to a funny moment on set.
Opposite: Detail from a teaser poster Dave Gibbons created for the 2007 Comic-Con in San Diego.

When Snyder set out to bring *Watchmen* to the big screen he felt very strongly about respecting the visual style of the graphic novel and handling it as nearly sacrosanct. "I always say treat *Watchmen* like an illuminated text, like it was written 2000 years ago," explains Snyder. "And that's how you should address the design." That message was heard and taken onboard by every member of the crew. Executive producer Herb Gains recalls, "Zack emphasized to everybody before they were hired the importance of being true to the novel and having that as a template, and as a bible, and as a point of reference." He goes on to explain, "Normally on films, you're doing all kinds of research and you're referencing all kinds of things... you're taking little bits and pieces of many different things and creating your world. But on this particularly, there was really one main reference."

Right: A concept drawing of Nite Owl II by comic book artist David Finch.

"Being true to the novel" included utilizing the secondary color palette wherever possible – on sets, costumes, vehicles, set dressing, and props. Production designer Alex McDowell, a veteran of such diverse productions as *Fight Club, Minority Report*, and Tim Burton's *Corpse Bride*, wholeheartedly embraced what he calls the original artists' "subversive thing." The twisting of the traditional comic book palette "...immediately made the entire *Watchmen* series into an incredibly striking-looking package, because people had not seen those juxtapositions of color," he says. This aesthetic choice played right into what McDowell was trying to achieve with his production design. He explains, "Using a controlled color palette is a great device in cinema, because it does that thing for the audience that is the equivalent of putting on tinted glasses. As soon as you enter the film space, the audience is encouraged to buy into the parallel nature of this world as opposed to their own experience."

"The thing people would always say about *Watchmen*, it's the unfilmable graphic novel because it's so dense. When you look at it, it looks like a phone book. But the story itself is pretty simple," says Snyder. The way Snyder and his crew went about achieving that density on the screen, without overcomplicating the narrative, was to maintain the same high degree of visual detail as the graphic novel. "One of the things that's great about working with Zack is that he is a fanatically interested in the fine detail and in finding the Easter eggs in all those implanted clues in the graphic novel, and pulling them out and layering them into the film," says McDowell. "It's going to be necessary to watch the film five, six, seven, or eight times to get all the depth."

The entire art department collaborated on rummaging through the graphic novel to grab visual elements that could be used to enhance each scene. Snyder recalls, "They did an amazing job, and it ended up being part of the thing that makes it such a complete world. Everyone loved it, and everyone approached it the same way, 'That's in the book. We need to make that.'" The fine details run the gamut from the bottle of Veidt hair spray Rorschach uses as a flamethrower on the SWAT team, to Nite Owl's autographed photo of the Twilight Lady. Sharp-eyed viewers should also be prepared to spot the four-legged chicken when Dan and Laurie dine at Rafael's (a sign of Dr. Manhattan's progressive effect on genetic engineering).

Finally, the filmmakers realized that within the book all action takes place within locations that are clearly delineated and instantly recognizable. The main characters, likewise, are sharply differentiated in terms of looks, build, posture, and manner of dress. In other words, the artists used very little of the generic when laying out the visual narrative. Understanding this relatively simple fact proved crucial to filming a story that spans almost fifty years and two planets. McDowell explains it from the perspective of design: "This film is interesting because the environments really have to represent the characters iconically, because you are in this very complex, fluid time stream back and forth..."

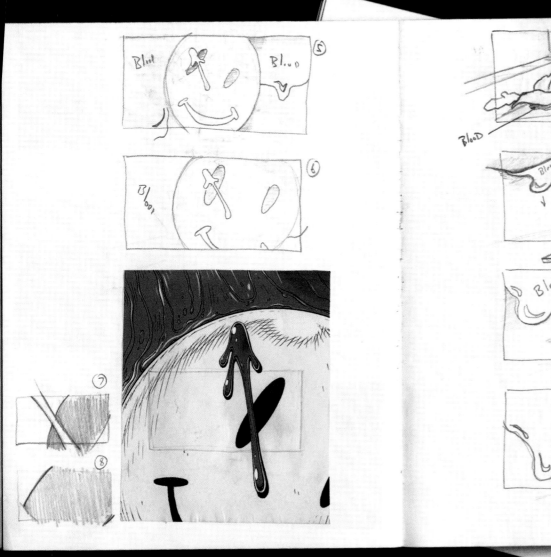

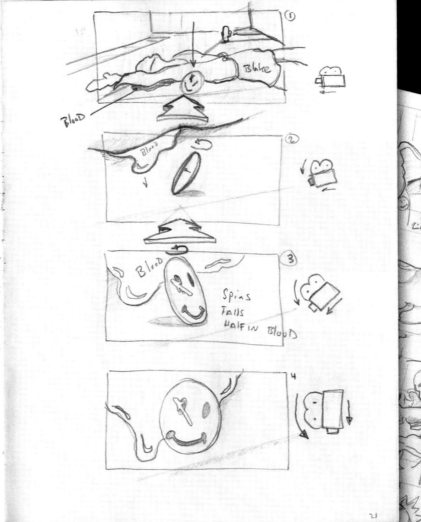

You need something to ground you when you cut back to something that's 1970 or '77 or '85." The surroundings are always unambiguous and there is no confusion when we flicker up and down the timeline, from Gila Flats in 1959, to the Minutemen headquarters in 1940, or to Laurie and Dr. Manhattan's apartment at Rockefeller Military Research Center in 1985.

All of these elements would contribute to creating an indefinable feeling that several crewmembers have described as "Watchmeny." But would they be enough on their own? The question remained as to how these elements would be combined, and what approach would be taken to put them on the screen.

Early on, internet rumors abounded that *Watchmen* would be a highly stylized film, heavily wrapped in computer-generated back-grounds, much like *Sin City* or Snyder's own 2007 smash hit *300*. What all of those cyberspace voices seemed to have forgotten was a central pillar of the original graphic novel. While it is true that the work is a deconstructionist satire of imperfect super heroes, un-checked power, and modern society, in order for any film based on all that to have the fullest impact possible, it is vitally important that the world projected feels absolutely real to the audience.

Above: *Storyboards by Zack Snyder.*

Snyder explains that despite "the satirical nature of the piece, it never lets you off the hook... It never winks at the camera. Its problems are real to it." From this he quickly realized, although both were graphic novels, *Watchmen* required an entirely different sort of graphic sensibility from *300*. "Pretty much from the start," he continues, "it felt like a physical movie."

Snyder got enthusiastic nods of assent about this key aesthetic from McDowell, costume designer Michael Wilkinson, and director of photography Larry Fong. "You can't stylize the form language in the way of the graphic novel," says McDowell. "You have to embed these characters in this real world and make them real. As a result, you're not doing what a conventional super-hero comic book movie might do, which is to push everything into fantasy. We're really trying to ground them in reality."

Concept art for Rorschach's entry into prison life, along with the finished shot from the film (above).

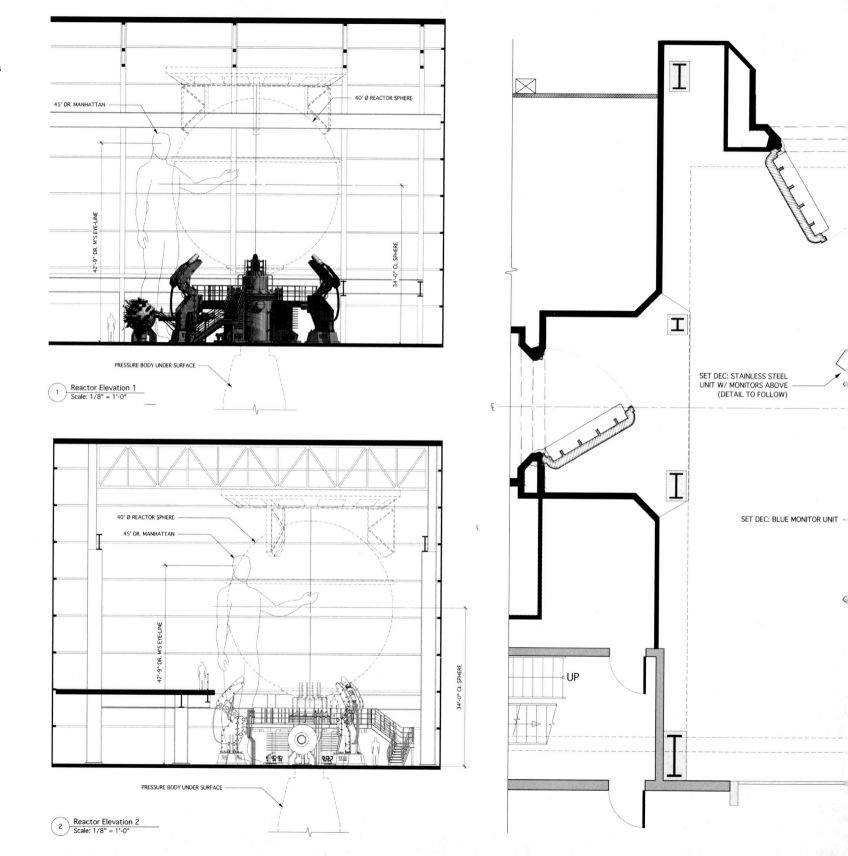

This spread: Elevation and floor plan blueprints for Dr. Manhattan's reactor lab.

Next spread: Concept drawing for Karnark, including interior and exterior details.

45' DR. MANHATTAN

40' Ø REACTOR SPHERE

42'-9" DR. M'S EYE-LINE

34'-0" CL SPHERE

PRESSURE BODY UNDER SURFACE

1 — Reactor Elevation 1
Scale: 1/8" = 1'-0"

40' Ø REACTOR SPHERE

45' DR. MANHATTAN

42'-9" DR. M'S EYE-LINE

34'-0" CL SPHERE

PRESSURE BODY UNDER SURFACE

2 — Reactor Elevation 2
Scale: 1/8" = 1'-0"

SET DEC: STAINLESS STEEL UNIT W/ MONITORS ABOVE (DETAIL TO FOLLOW)

SET DEC: BLUE MONITOR UNIT

UP

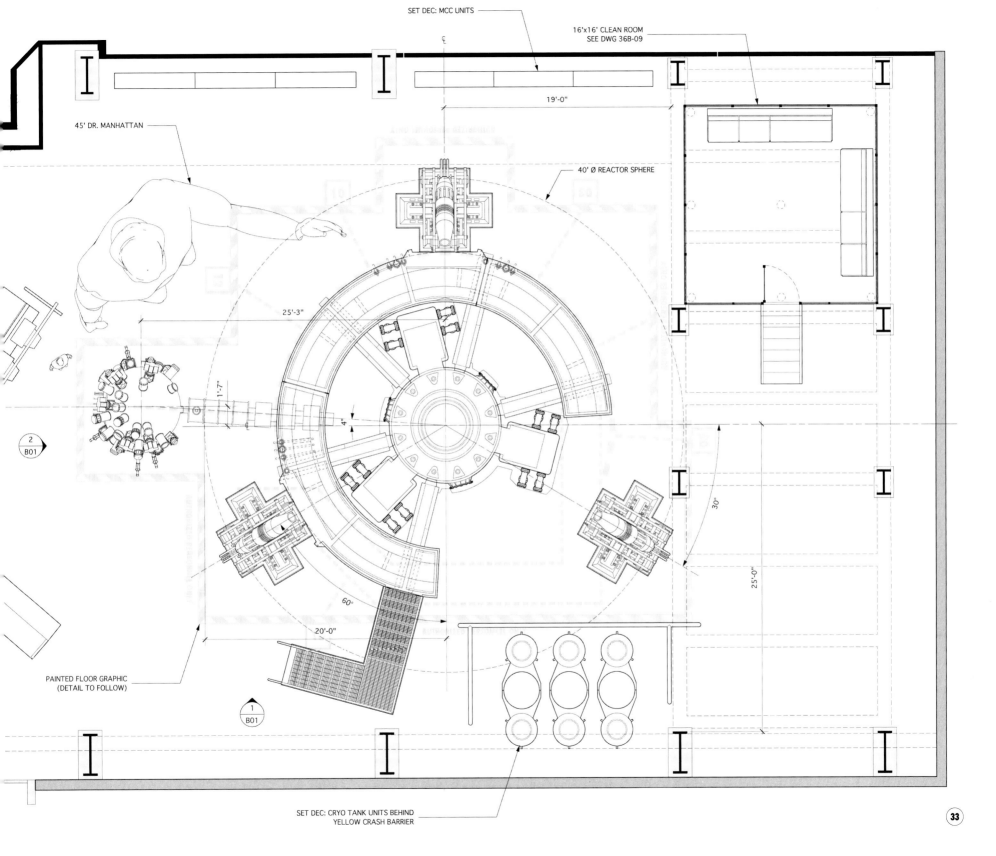

SET DEC: MCC UNITS

16'x16' CLEAN ROOM
SEE DWG 36B-09

19'-0"

45' DR. MANHATTAN

40' Ø REACTOR SPHERE

25'-3"

1'-7"

4°

2
B01

30°

25'-0"

60°

20'-0"

PAINTED FLOOR GRAPHIC
(DETAIL TO FOLLOW)

1
B01

SET DEC: CRYO TANK UNITS BEHIND
YELLOW CRASH BARRIER

33

Naturally, any film that features an enormous clockwork glass palace floating across the surface of Mars and a 200-foot blue man-god striding through the jungles of Vietnam is going to rely at least somewhat on CGI to tell its story. Visitors to any of the shooting locations in and around Vancouver, British Columbia, however, would have been far more likely to hear the sounds of nail guns and circular saws than to see grips rigging up green screens. Locations would eventually include an abandoned paper mill and a lumberyard, transformed by construction crews in a matter of months into everything from Dr. Manhattan's lab, to the prison where Rorschach is held, to Hollis Mason's garage. In nearly every scene, there would be a concrete, tangible reality in which the actors could physically bring their characters to life.

One of the sources that Snyder drew inspiration from, for both environments and filming style, was Martin Scorsese's classic 1976 film of vigilante justice on the streets of New York City, *Taxi Driver*. "Zack and I, in the very first meeting, we started talking about how to get the language of the graphic novel onto the screen," recalls McDowell. "And *Taxi Driver* came up in the very early conversations. And for me that was real key to see that it's kind of a stylized film, but a location-based film, shot in New York. It's the right period, and it has the right degree of gritty punch."

THE COMEDIAN.
WATCHMEN

#6

#5

BLAKE READING PAPER
WATCHMEN HQ 1970
FRONT PAGE

#4
VEIDT'S DESK Oct 14 1985

#3
VEIDT LOBBY Oct 1985

#2
MOLOCH'S APARTMENT 1985
FRONT PAGE

FINAL — The New York Gazette
RUSS HAVE A-BOMB

FINAL — The New York Gazette
SOVIETS CALL M. 'IMPERIALIST WEAPON'
President Nixon Responds with Public Statement

OPTION 1

FINAL — The New York Gazette
DOOMSDAY CLOCK AT 5 TO MIDNIGHT
Experts Warn of Imminent Danger
Geneva Talks, U.S. Refuses to Discuss Dr. Manhattan

MORNING EDITION — The New York Gazette
AFGHANISTAN STRONG HOLDS DISCOVERED
Soviet Troop Buildup Prompts Swift Reaction from Western Powers

FINAL — The New York Gazette
SOVIETS WILL NOT TOLERATE U ADVENTURISM IN AFGHANIS

FINAL — The New York Gazette
CRIMINAL WORLD GOES GA-GA OVER
SILK SPECTRE

Los Angeles Times
Soviets Escalate Nuclear Warhead Production

VICTORY!
★★★★
JAPAN SURRENDERS
The New York Gazette
THE END OF WAR

NEW FRONTIERSMAN
★★★★
HONOR IS LIKE THE HAWK: SOMETIMES IT MUST GO HOODED
RED ARMAGEDDON

NEW YORK POST — METRO
COPS SAY 'LET THEM DO IT'
"Keene Act" bans all vigilantism

SPECIAL EDITION: LATE-BREAKING NEW
NEW YORK POST — METRO
WAR?

All events point to global war
- Escalation in number of troops
- Massive revolts reported
- National Guard called to aid
STORIES ON PAGE 2

PROPS

PAGE 1 OF 2

EXPRESS

HOW SICK IS DICK!

Nostalgia

PAGE 2 OF 2

WAR?

The New York Gazette

RSCHACH REVEALED

The New York Gazette

SOVIETS INVADE AFGHANISTAN

RENT CONTROLS TO BE STUDIED

FINAL ★★★★★

The New York Gazette

Weather
Sunny and cool today; increasing cloudiness tonight. Tomorrow; mostly cloudy with a chance of rain. Details on page 31.

VOL. CXXXV No. 46,576   Copyright © 1985 The New York Gazette Company   NEW YORK, FRIDAY, NOVEMBER 1, 1985   ★★★   30 CENTS

SOVIETS INVADE AFGHANISTAN

Stage Set for Genocide

By WILLIAM BALL
Special to The New York Gazette

WASHINGTON - The US and Britain had a quick response to the Soviet action taking place in Afghanistan. The White House called a Press Conference with President Nixon addressing the media on the question of military retaliation to the growing number of troops on the Afghanistan Pakistan border. The area know as the Frontier is a lawless stronghold of terrorism that cannot be tolerated. London backed President Nixon with his resolve to send troops to the region and urged the European powers to show solidarity in dealing with the Russian government. Relations with Russia were further complicated when the Pakistan government denied that support was building among the military Generals who have influence on the Tribal Leaders of the region.

Lawless Stronghold of Terrorism

AThe US and Britain agreed that they would not make concessions to the Soviets but they were split badly over the question of punishment. The US is frustrated that the Soviets have escaped retribution in the past and are seeking firmer action in the way of concessions. London was less insistent, perhaps because they have a much longer good term relationship with the Soviet Regime. Another issue is the fragile state of the Afghanistan economic problems as

well as a persistent challenge from Muslim fundamentalists.

Trying to keep Nixon out of the fray, his aides made no changes to his public appearances and Nixon is due to speak to the Congress the following day.

Senior US intelligence sources confirmed that Soviet troop movement has been building for weeks with tanks amassed in the major areas around Kabul and the Khyber Pass.

The Kremlin is denying the report and has issued a statement denouncing any involvement in the affairs of the Afghanistan government.

Kruschev has not been seen in the public eye for quiet some time now and is rumored to be recovering from a bout of alcoholism in his dacha in the southern Georgia woods of the Ukraine. Tass has made mention in the Soviet papers of the escalation of tensions but continued to take shots at Nixon's worsening image among the voters over the economic decline now plaguing the US economy. US patience is beginning to wear thin. At a hearing of the Senate Foreign Relations Committee, Secretary of State, Henry Kissinger called on the Kremlin to "stop lying."

"They Have Done Everything To Mislead Us"

Administration officials would not reveal what the next step is. Kissinger informed the President at about midday that there might be a possible intercept of a convoy. The rules of any engagement would be discussed between Kissinger and the President and the rules laid out in principle to the move and provided "one or two elements of guidance on the concept were agreed upon" the situation could proceed. By that Kissinger implied that apparently US intervention by force may be applied.

"They have done everything to mislead us about the location of their troops and the intention of the build up."

The final decision will rest with the President when the Presidential party returns to Washington aboard Air Force One next Tuesday.

The Afghanistan diplomat abruptly left a staff discussion of the upcoming Geneva summit and entered into private discussions with

Soviet Military Helicopters landing in Kabul today. Thousands more Russian troops entered the country via tanks and armoured military convoys. Analysts predict the Russians are planning a long occupation.

RENT CONTROLS TO BE STUDIED

City Forms Panel For Businesses' Interests

By M. J. GEISTHARDT
Special to The New York Gazette

The mayor of New York City, joined by some council members, yesterday announced the formation of a commission to find out why the hell everybody is working so hard on this movie. The mayor of New York City, joined by some council members, yesterday announced the formation of a commission to find out why the hell everybody is working so hard on this movie.

The study is the initiative of the mayor who many believe to have strong ties to business. The mayor of New York City, joined by some council members, yesterday announced the formation of a commission to find out why the hell everybody is working so hard on this movie. The mayor of New York City, joined by some council members, yesterday announced the formation of a commission to find out why the hell everybody is working so hard on this movie. The mayor of New York City, joined by some council members, yesterday announced the formation of a commission to find out why the hell everybody is working so hard on this movie. The mayor of New

Major Holdings in Tudor City Are Being Sold

By LEON BUCKLEY
Special to The New York Gazette

MANHATTAN - The real estate entrepreneurs Harry B. Helmer and Artie Schwartz has signed an agreement to sell their remaining properties in Tudor City on the East Side of Manhattan for an undisclosed price of two buyers who said they were considering converting the apartments into cooperatives.

Agreement to Sell

The sale involves 6 of 13 large apartment buildings in Tudor City, 4 brownstones and the land under the 2 parks in the complex. For many years the efforts by Mr. Helmer and Mr. Schwartz to build apartment towers on the two parks they own in Tudor City have been frustrated by tenants, city agencies and courts.

The real estate entrepreneurs Harry B. Helmer and Artie Schwartz has signed an agreement to sell their remaining properties in Tudor City on the East Side of Manhattan for an undisclosed price of two buyers who said they were considering converting the apartments into cooperatives. The sale involves 6 of 13 large apartment buildings in Tudor City, 4 brownstones and the land

Frustration Cited

For many years the efforts by Mr. Helmer and Mr. Schwartz to build apartment towers on the two parks they own in Tudor City have been frustrated by tenants, city agencies and courts. The real estate entrepreneurs Harry B. Helmer and Artie Schwartz has signed an agreement to sell their remaining properties in Tudor City on the East Side of Manhattan for an undisclosed price of two buyers who said they were considering converting the apartments into cooperatives.

The sale involves 6 of 13 large apartment buildings in Tudor City, 4 brownstones and the land under the 2 parks in the complex. For many years the efforts by Mr. Helmer and Mr. Schwartz to build apartment towers on the two parks they own in Tudor City have been frustrated by tenants, city agencies and courts.

The real estate entrepreneurs Harry B. Helmer and Artie Schwartz has signed an agreement to sell their remaining properties in Tudor City on the East Side of Manhattan for an undisclosed price of two buyers who said they were considering

Continued on Page Three, Column d

State to Widen Role of Judge in Picking Jury

By ROBERT K. STEVENS
The New York Gazette

ALBANY - Legislative leaders have agreed on a measure to permit judges to take over the main role in questioning prospective jurors in new York courts. The measure would amend current law to curb a power long cherished by lawyers and would put into effect a system that Wallace Craig the state judge has urged.

The measure would not exclude lawyers from questioning; rather it would put all judges in charge of the questioning and encourage them to circumscribe the lawyer's role. Legislative leaders have agreed on a measure to permit judges to take over the main role in questioning prospective jurors in new York courts. The measure would amend current law to curb a power long cherished by lawyers and would put into effect a system that Wallace Craig the state judge has urged.

The measure would not exclude lawyers from questioning; rather it would put all judges in charge of the questioning and encourage them to circumscribe the lawyer's role. Legislative leaders have agreed on a measure to permit judges to

take over the main role in questioning prospective jurors in new York courts.

The measure would amend current law to curb a power long cherished by lawyers and would put into effect a system that Wallace Craig the state judge has urged.

The measure would not exclude lawyers from questioning; rather it would put all judges in charge of the questioning and encourage them to circumscribe the lawyer's role. Legislative leaders have agreed on a measure to permit judges to take over the main role in questioning prospective jurors in new York courts.

The measure would amend current law to curb a power long cherished by lawyers and would put into effect a system that Wallace Craig the state judge has urged.

The measure would not exclude lawyers from questioning; rather it would put all judges in charge of the questioning and encourage them to circumscribe the lawyer's role.

Legislative leaders have agreed on a measure to permit judges to

Continued on Page Five, Column 2

HUNGARIAN LEADER VISITS LONDON

By LEON BUCKLEY
Special to The New York Gazette

LONDON - Janos Kadar, the Hungarian Communist Party leader, arrived in London today for a three-day official visit that will include talks with Prime Minister Margaret Thatcher.

British officials say the visit is part of Mrs. Thatcher's effort to encourage discussions with the Eastern bloc nations.

The Hungarian Communist Party leader, arrived in London today for a three-day official visit that will include talks with Prime Minister Margaret Thatcher. British officials say the visit is part of Mrs. Thatcher's effort to encourage discussions with the Eastern bloc nations.

Measure Will Not Exclude Lawyers

Legislative leaders have agreed on a measure to permit judges to take over the main role in questioning prospective jurors in new York courts. The measure would amend current law to curb a power long cherished by lawyers and would put into effect a system that Wallace Craig the state judge has urged.

The measure would not exclude lawyers from questioning; rather it would put all judges in charge of the questioning and encourage them to circumscribe the lawyer's role.

Legislative leaders have agreed on a measure to permit judges to take over the main role in questioning prospective jurors in new York courts.

The measure would amend current law to curb a power long cherished by lawyers and would put into effect a system that Wallace Craig the state judge has urged.

The measure would not exclude lawyers from questioning; rather it would put all judges in charge of the questioning and encourage them to circumscribe the lawyer's role.

The Hungarian Communist Party leader, arrived in London today for a three-day official visit that will include talks with Prime Minister Margaret Thatcher. British officials say the visit is part of Mrs. Thatcher's

Continued on Page Two, Column 5

TRACKING THE RUSSIANS

Some Defectors Join Afghan Rebels

By R. E. KLINGHOFFER
Special to The New York Gazette

WASHINGTON - The US and Britain agreed that they would not make concessions to the Soviets but they were split badly over the question of punishment. The US is frustrated that the Soviets have escaped retribution in the past and are seeking firmer action in the way of concessions. London was less insistent, perhaps because they have a much longer good term relationship with the Soviet Regime. Another issue is the fragile state of the Afghanistan economic problems as well as a persistent challenge from Muslim fundamentalists.

Movement Building for Weeks

Trying to keep Nixon out of the fray, his aides made no changes to his public appearances and Nixon is due to speak to the Congress the following day. Senior US intelligence sources confirmed that Soviet troop movement has been building for weeks with tanks amassed in the major areas around Kabul and the Khyber Pass.

The Kremlin is denying the report and has issued a statement denouncing any involvement in the affairs of the Afghanistan government.

Kruschev has not been seen in the public eye for quiet some time now and is rumored to be recovering from a bout of alcoholism in his dacha in the southern Georgia woods of the Ukraine. Tass has made mention in the Soviet papers of the escalation of tensions but continued to take shots at Nixon's worsening image among the voters over the economic decline now plaguing the US economy.

Next Step Unknown

US patience is beginning to wear thin. At a hearing of the Senate Foreign Relations Committee, Secretary of State, Henry Kissinger called on the Kremlin to "stop lying."

"They have done everything to mislead us about the location of their troops and the intention of the build up. Administration officials would not reveal what the next step is. Kissinger informed the President at about midday that there might be a possible intercept of a convoy. The rules of any engagement would be discussed between Kissinger and the President and the rules laid out in principle to the move and provided "one or two elements of guidance on the concept were agreed upon" the situation could proceed. By that Kissinger implied that apparently US intervention by force may be applied.

The final decision will rest with the President when the Presidential party returns to Washington aboard Air Force One next Tuesday.

The Afghanistan diplomat abruptly left a staff discussion of

Continued on Page Two, Column 2

INSIDE

Rescue Efforts Continue
Search efforts continue for survivors of the massive mudslide which hit Puerto Rico last month. It is still unclear how so many people are missing or dead. Page 15

Ozone Fears Revealed in Studies
Scientists Farman, Gardiner and Shanklin released another report of their discovery of an ozone hole over Antarctica. Page 29

Continued on Page Two, Column 5

Much of the insight *Taxi Driver* provided was in terms of camera angles and lighting cues to achieve a raw, natural look, but it also provided reference for a city that has seen better days. "Rundown" and "seedy" became virtues to be emulated. "The balance is when you have an all-purple building – how does it stop looking like a comic book building?" asks McDowell. "We've done that with a very considered history of aging and layering." The result was a very tattered and dog-eared New York, steeped in the *Watchmen* aesthetic, but familiar enough to be entirely believable and even slightly disturbing.

The acid test came when co-creator Gibbons was scheduled to take a tour of the sets. "When Dave arrived," recalls Snyder, "I think we all were a bit afraid, and excited at the same time, because… you never know." But writing about that visit to the set, Gibbons sounds more than pleased with the way his work has been translated: "I'm overwhelmed by the depth and detail of what I'm seeing. But more than that. I'm overwhelmed by the commitment, the passion, the palpable desire to do this right. I'm starting to feel a glow that eclipses even Dr. Manhattan's…"

Snyder admits he found Gibbon's enthusiastic reaction reassuring. "You could show it to a fan boy, and he just says, 'Yeah, those are cool statues,' or, 'The Owlship looks awesome.' But it's another thing entirely when the creator of that thing sees it and goes, 'Wow. You guys loved that, didn't you? It shows.' I don't think I'll get that experience again." He continues, "I feel like we're trying to push all the design to the very edge… So, maybe when we make our pictures, they're going to be something you've never seen. And I think that's a reason to go to the movies."

Previous spread: Over four decades of newspaper headlines.

Above: The Comedian's .45.
Right: Hollis Mason's living room.

CONCEPT ART

Long before a single foot of film rolls, the actors step out of their trailers, or a dab of paint touches the first set, designers and illustrators – with input from the director – work to define every aspect of the look of a film. It is an organic process, moving from the very general to the very specific through months of collaboration. "You go through a conceptual research phase, where you set the world. Then you go through a conceptual phase where you start illustrating the feel of the world. Then you have a design phase where you start locking down the structure," production designer Alex McDowell explains.

As mentioned, the filmmakers relied heavily on the graphic novel as a visual reference. Still, that left them a significant degree of freedom in hammering out the exact details only hinted at in the fine-line drawing of the original panels. What texture should Ozymandias's costume have? What size and shape should the reactor in Dr. Manhattan's lab be? The script provided a preliminary sorting of what environments, costumes, and props would be included in the film, and allowed initial planning to begin. What became the real blueprints for constructing the onscreen world, however, were the shot-by-shot storyboards drawn up by Zack Snyder himself.

The entire art department found the boards added a refreshing transparency to the creative process that fostered both freedom and teamwork. "I've never worked with a director who's drawn the entire movie from beginning to end, and that speaks to his clarity of vision. We move forward with decisions that are being driven by the narrative and by Zack's boards and by the graphic novel, and Zack has almost never said, 'No, I'm seeing it differently.' It's a really great, symbiotic, collaborative way of working," McDowell says.

"[Snyder's] drawings are simple, but they're full of detail. They're drawn quickly, but they're very specific," McDowell points out. The crew quickly realized that there was reasoning behind every little facet Snyder had included in these rough sketches. "When they hinge a door on the set, they should hinge it the way it's drawn. It should open this way, not that way, 'cause when it opens, it exposes a thing," Snyder explains. "It's a house of cards, you know? If you take one thing out, sometimes the scene doesn't work."

The storyboards were also a crucial reference for the main title sequence, a montage of how the history of the 20th Century might have flowed if masked heroes had really existed. Although panels and dialogue from the graphic novel inspired some of the shots in the sequence, many – such as the bomber Miss Jupiter dropping the A-bomb on Hiroshima, or Dr. Manhattan being present at the Apollo moon landing – were entirely new imaginings of events in the Watchmen world and needed to be carefully thought out.

Along with the storyboards, reference images, and pages from the novel, when the concept illustrations and location photos began rolling in, they were posted in a conference space at the production offices dubbed the "War Room." It served as a forum where the crew as a whole could view the art and talk about the film. McDowell explains, "It's really a vital part of how we planned the film, so that we could get the graphic novel layers… Almost in every set we have a frame or several frames from the graphic novel." He adds, "It's an organic expression of the development of the visual language for the film – probably to a larger extent than I've ever done on a film."

RORSCHACH.
WATCHMEN
DESIGNED BY MICHAEL WILKINSON.

This spread: Various views of the production design "War Room."

Above: The cast reads through the script in the "War Room."

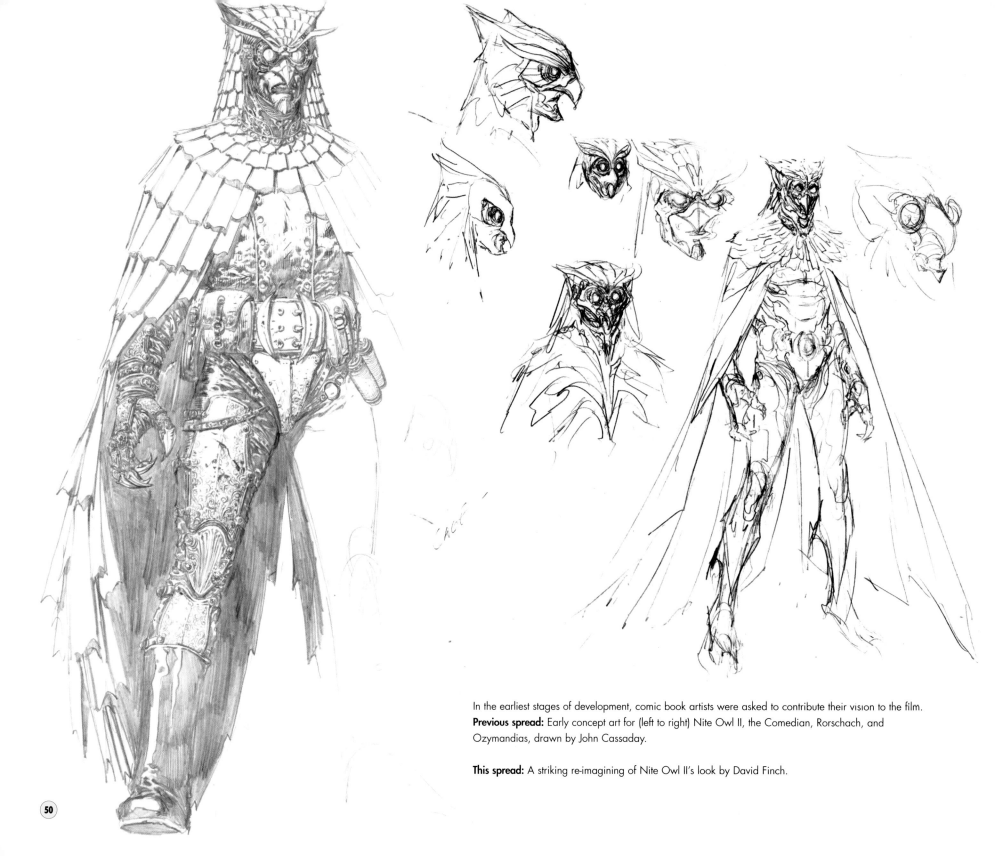

In the earliest stages of development, comic book artists were asked to contribute their vision to the film.
Previous spread: Early concept art for (left to right) Nite Owl II, the Comedian, Rorschach, and Ozymandias, drawn by John Cassaday.

This spread: A striking re-imagining of Nite Owl II's look by David Finch.

David Finch's versions of (left to right) the Owlship, Silk Spectre II, and Ozymandias.

Adam Hughes' sketches of (left to right) Nite Owl II, Silk Spectre II, the Comedian, and Ozymandias.

Right and below: Zack Snyder's storyboards for the moment Edward Blake is thrown to his death, with a final shot from the film.

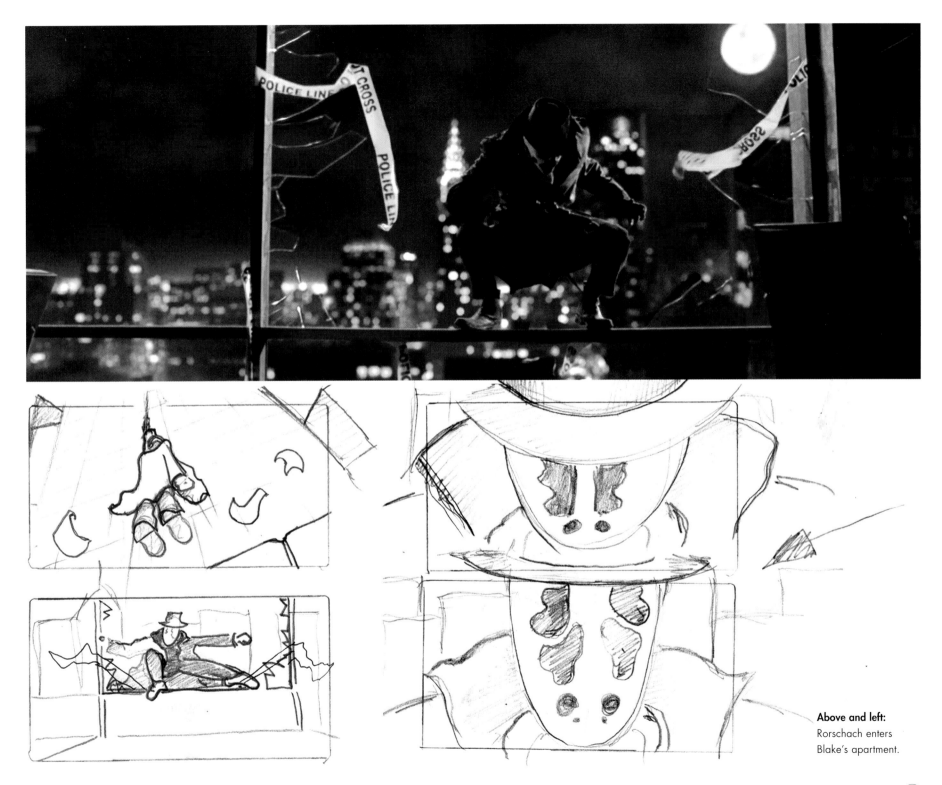

Above and left:
Rorschach enters
Blake's apartment.

This spread and next spread: Excerpts from Snyder's storyboards for the events leading up to Rorschach's capture. As a SWAT team enter Moloch's building, Rorschach makes use of a can of Veidt For Men Hair Spray.

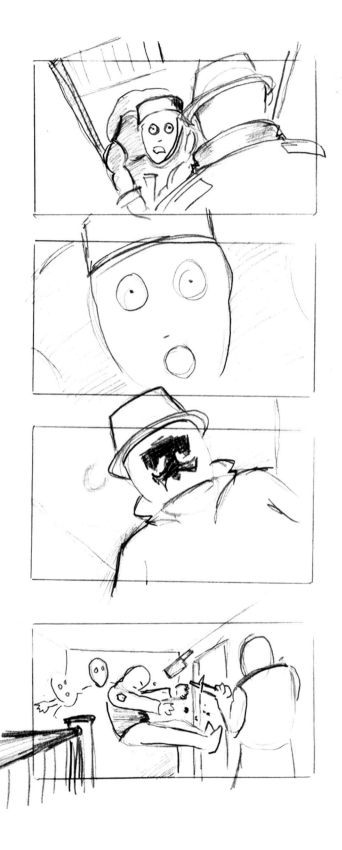

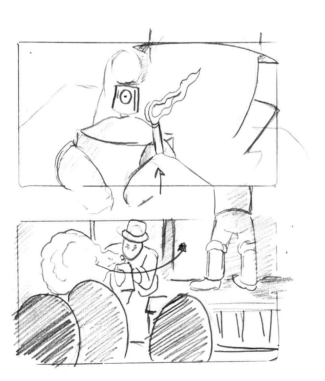

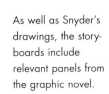

As well as Snyder's drawings, the story-boards include relevant panels from the graphic novel.

After grappling with
the armed policemen,
Rorschach makes a
run for the window...

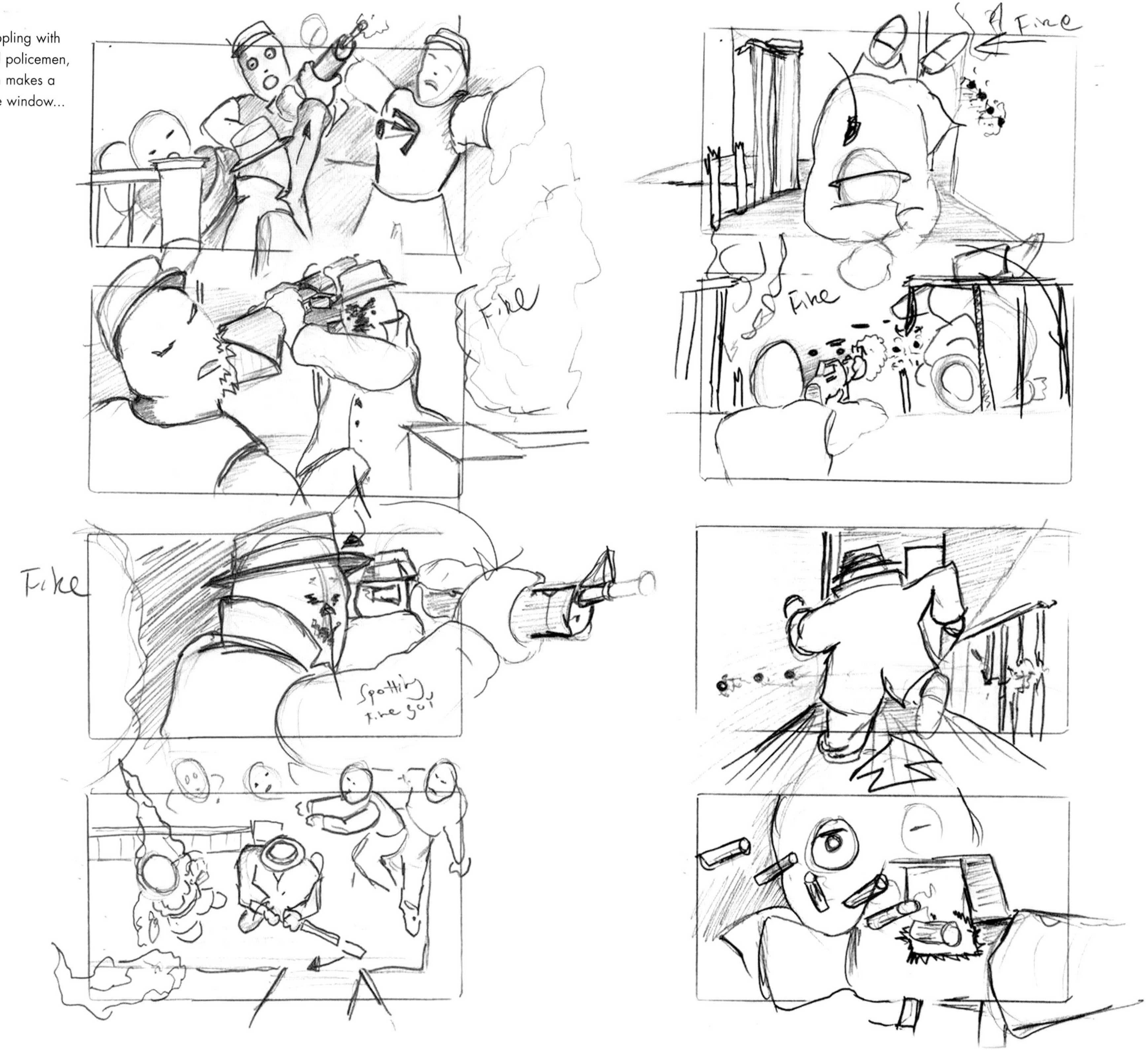

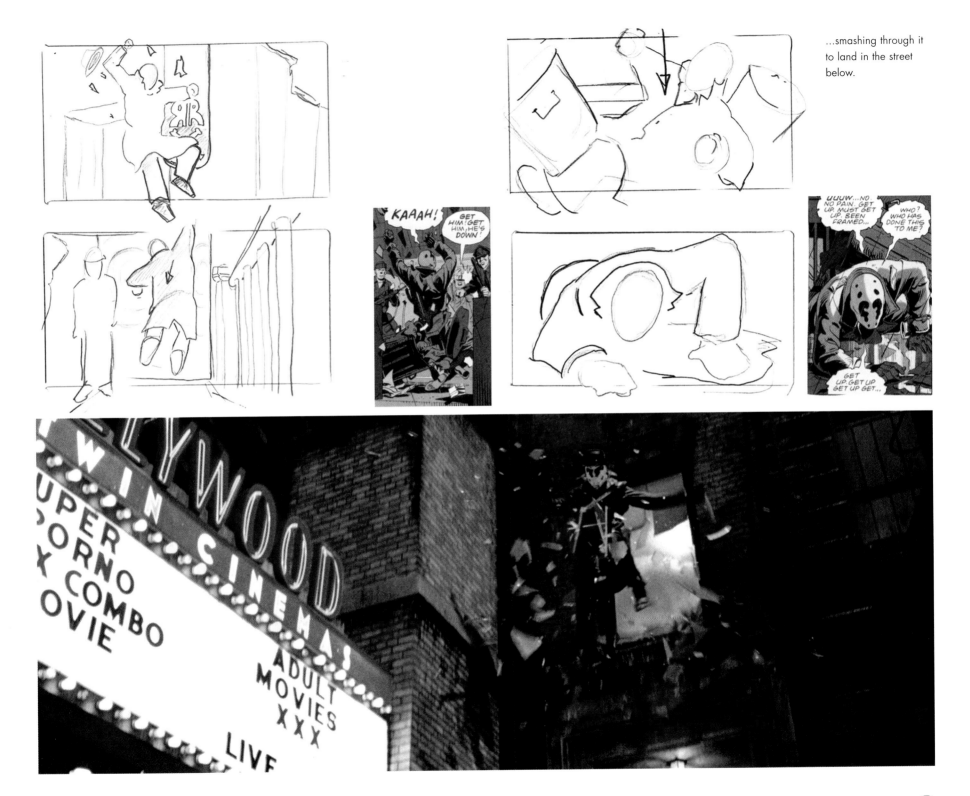

...smashing through it to land in the street below.

KAAAH!

GET HIM! GET HIM, HE'S DOWN!

UUUW...NO NO PAIN...GET UP. MUST GET UP. BEEN FRAMED...

WHO? WHO HAS DONE THIS TO ME?

GET UP. GET UP GET UP GET...

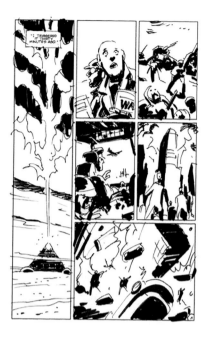

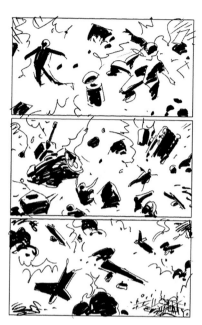

This spread: Artist Dave Gibbons and original *Watchmen* colorist John Higgins give us a taste of what the graphic novel's climax might have looked like if Adrian Veidt had followed the film's script. These new "pages" were drawn at Zack Snyder's request during pre-production, to ensure that the film's re-imagined ending nevertheless drew from an authentic source. Just as he did for the original series, Gibbons drew thumbnail sketches of each page before moving on to the full-size art.

Next spread: After filming had been completed, Gibbons also drew new illustrations of some key shots from the film, for marketing and licensing purposes. (Colors again by John Higgins.)

WHY THE *HELL* DIDN'T WE GET A *LAUNCH DETECTION*?

IT'S NOT THE *SOVIETS*, SIR -- INTEL INDICATES THE *ENERGY SIGNATURE* WAS GENERATED BY DR. *MANHATTAN*!

B

C

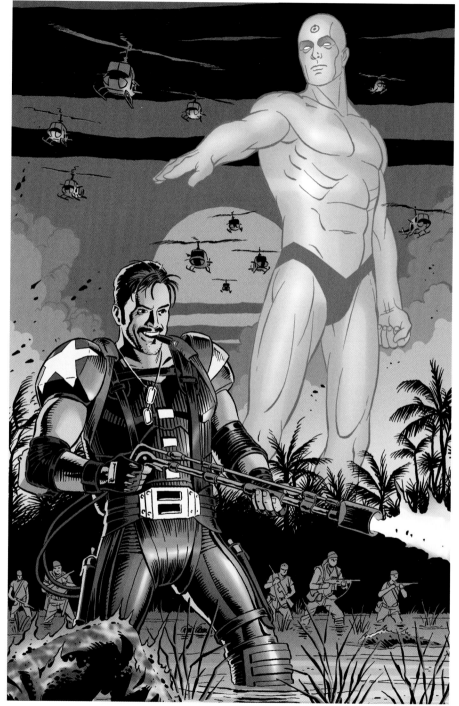

THE
END
IS
NIGH

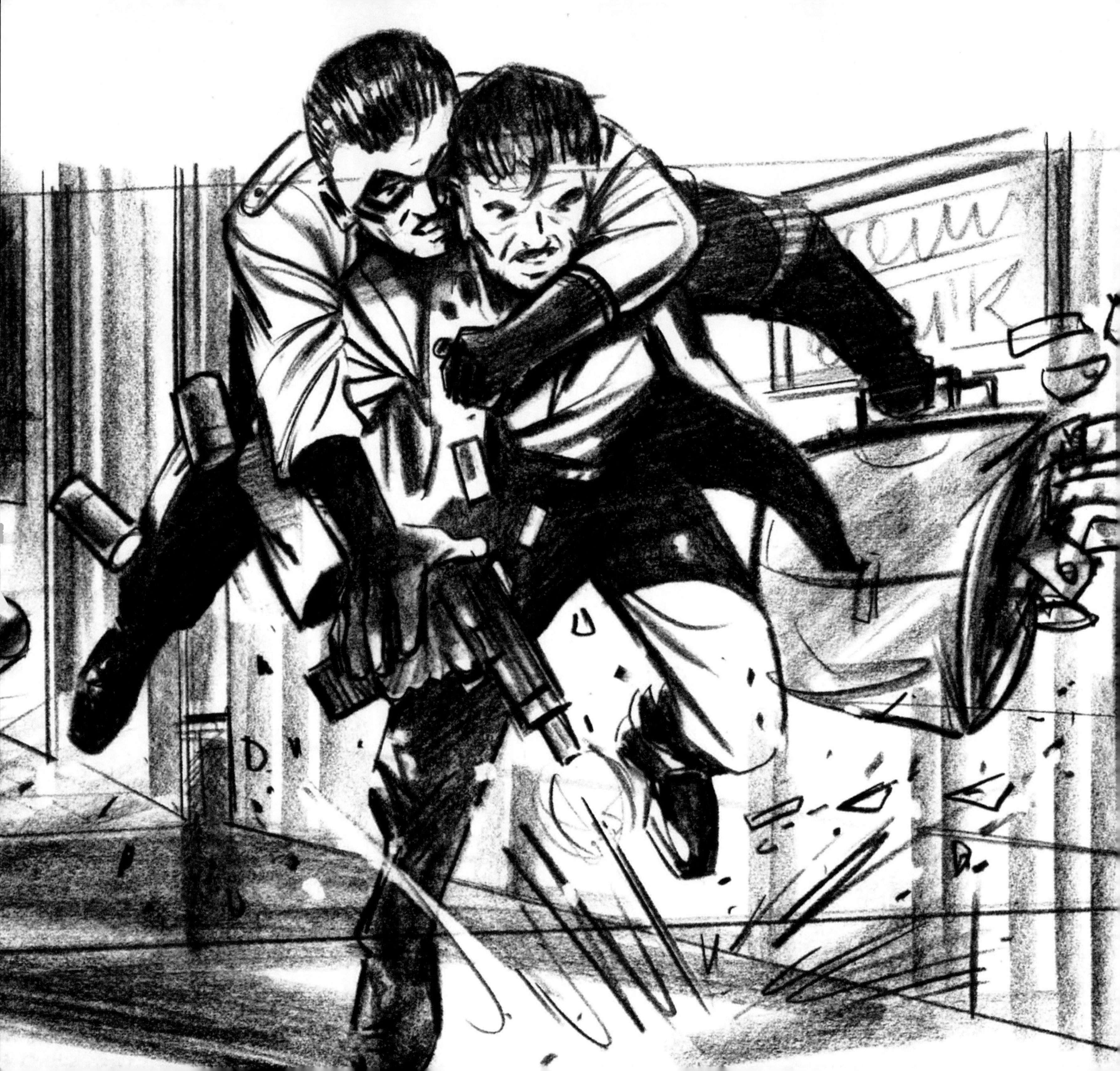

Above and right: Silk Spectre I drinks in the adoration of her fans.

Opposite: Concept for the "Miss Jupiter" carrying out the bombing of Hiroshima by artist Dan Milligan.

Above: A pin-up of Sally Jupiter in the Vargas style by artist James Jean.

Right: Concept sketch of Sally posing for a war bond poster by "Normal" Rockwell.

This spread: Sally Jupiter, AKA Silk Spectre I, lends her beauty and brawn to the war effort in deleted scenes intended for the opening credit sequence.

Next spread: Concept for the original "Watchmen" meeting. **Next spread opposite:** The Minutemen, 1940 (left to right): Silhouette (Apollonia Vanova), Mothman (Niall Matter), Dollar Bill (Dan Payne), Nite Owl I (Clint Carleton), Captain Metropolis (Darryl Scheelar), the Comedian (Jeffrey Dean Morgan, kneeling), Silk Spectre I (Carla Gugino), Hooded Justice (Glenn Ennis).

Opposite: Concepts for the Comedian single-handedly raising the flag on Mt. Suribachi; Silhouette celebrating VJ Day; Einstein weeping over footage of the atom bomb; young Walter Kovacs confronted with his mother's line of work.

Above: Dollar Bill learns too late the disadvantages of a cape.
Below: Mothman loses it.

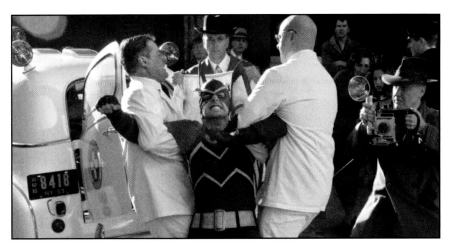

Above and below: Pregnant with Laurie, Sally Jupiter has one last supper with the gang. Concept work by artist Dan Milligan.

One small step for Dr. Manhattan, one giant leap for mankind.

PRODUCTION ART

Previous spread: Nite Owl II and the Comedian confront an ugly mob during the Police Strike Riots of '77.

This spread: Silk Spectre II drops in to help folks out of a burning tenement.

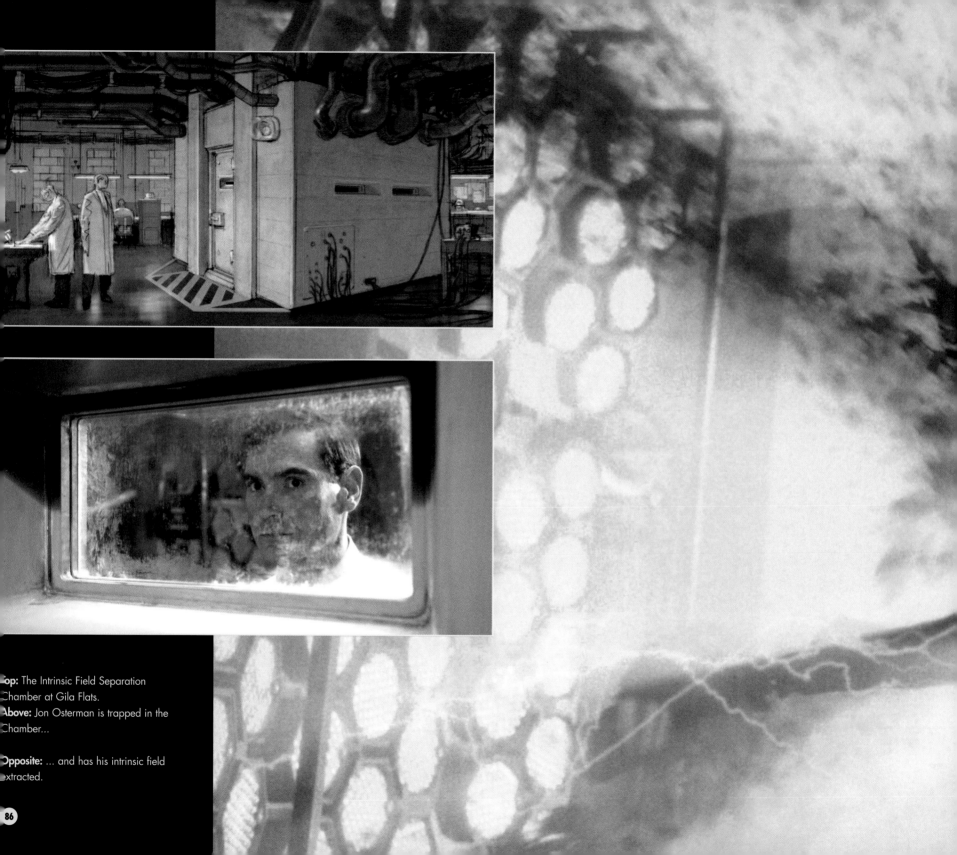

Top: The Intrinsic Field Separation
Chamber at Gila Flats.
Above: Jon Osterman is trapped in the
Chamber...

Opposite: ... and has his intrinsic field
extracted.

After his accident, Jon Osterman, the son of a watchmaker, reassembles himself piece by piece until he is reborn in the lunch room.

This spread: Dr. Manhattan does his country's bidding in Vietnam, but becomes increasingly detached from humanity.

Next spread: Hundreds of Viet Cong surrender to Dr. Manhattan personally.

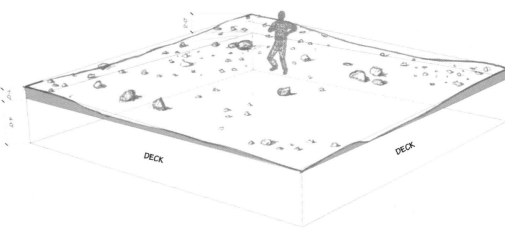

This spread: Concepts and elements for digitally constructing Mars and Dr. Manhattan's clockwork glass palace.

Next spread: The palace rises from the surface of the red planet, from wireframe to final shot.

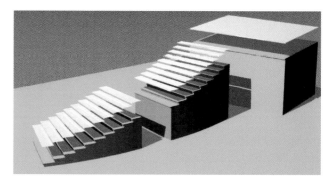

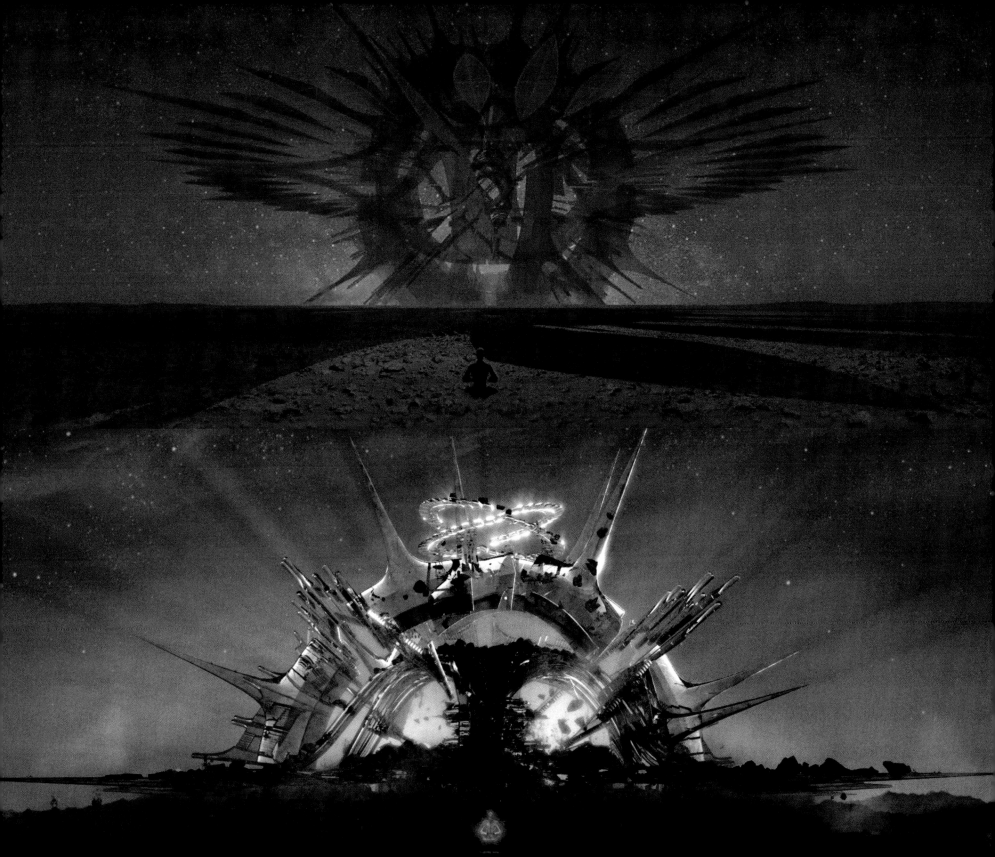

Veidt Enterprises headquarters takes shape in midtown Manhattan.

The cemetery for Edward Blake's funeral.

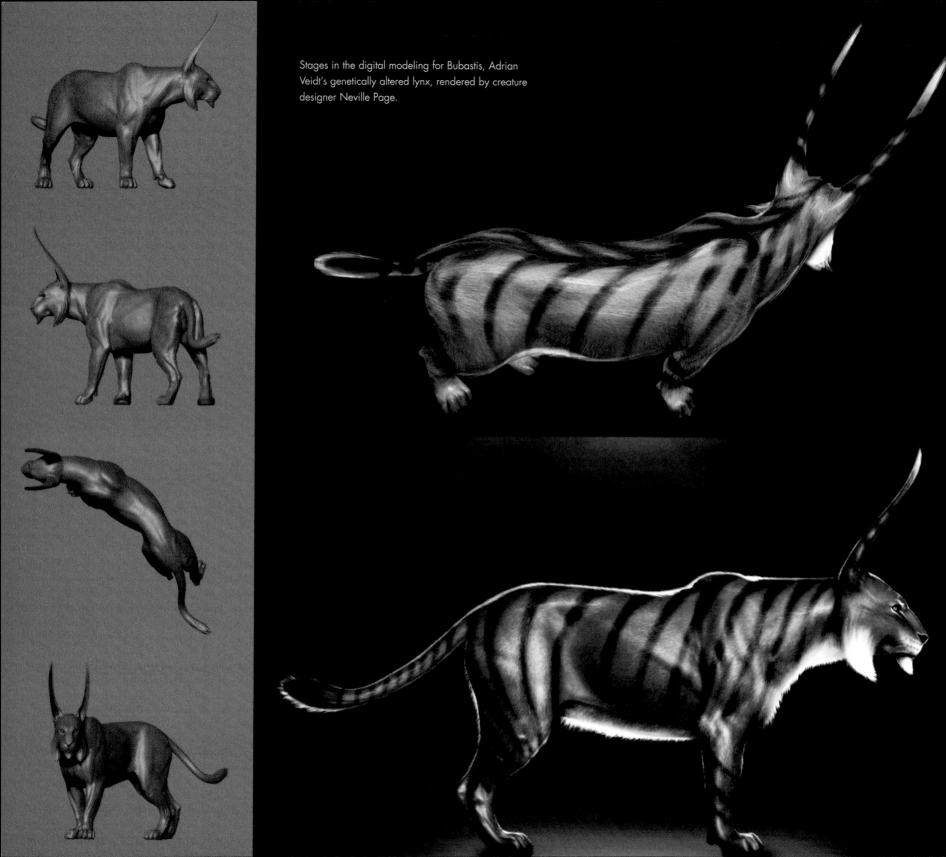

Stages in the digital modeling for Bubastis, Adrian Veidt's genetically altered lynx, rendered by creature designer Neville Page.

Concept of the Owlship approaching Veidt's Antarctic retreat, Karnak.

SETS

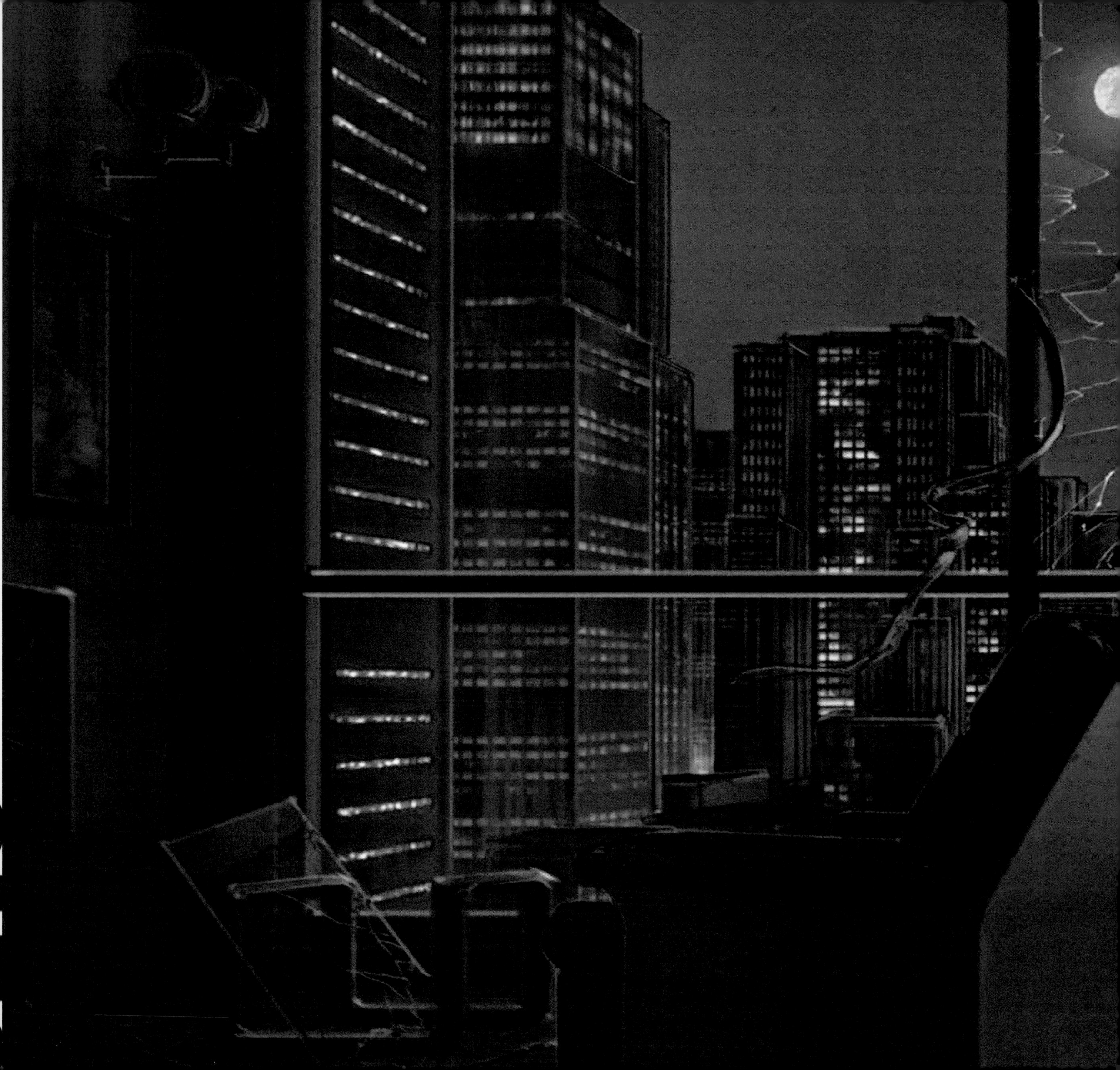

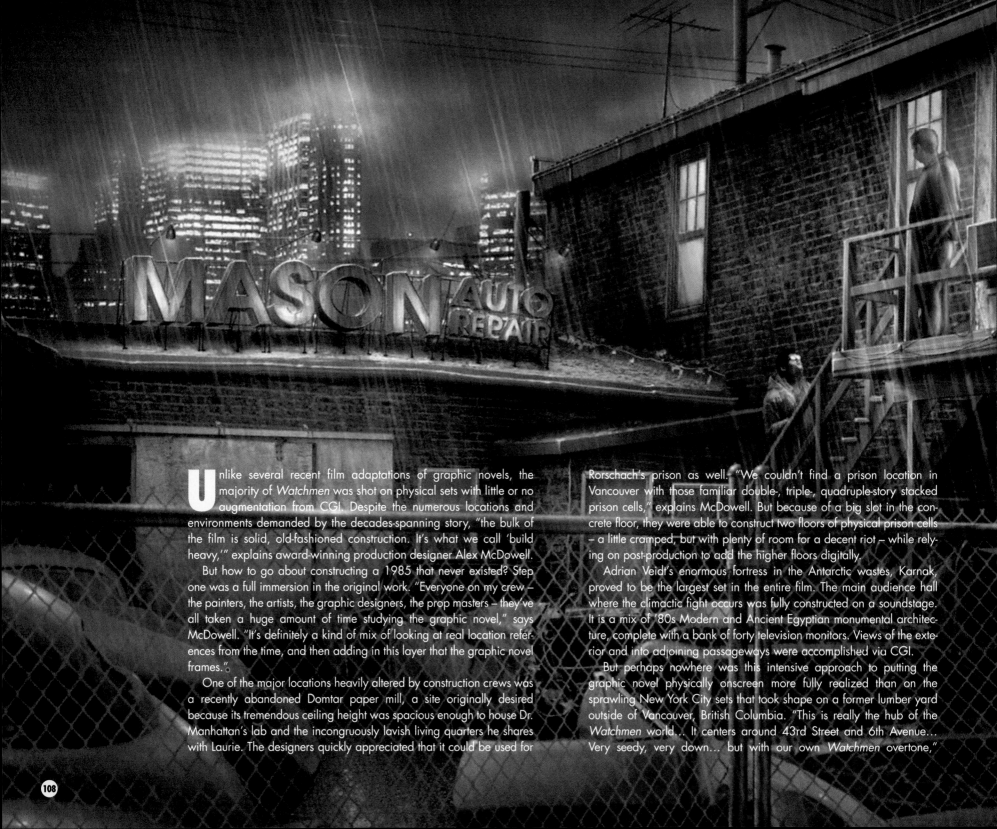

nlike several recent film adaptations of graphic novels, the majority of *Watchmen* was shot on physical sets with little or no augmentation from CGI. Despite the numerous locations and environments demanded by the decades-spanning story, "the bulk of the film is solid, old-fashioned construction. It's what we call 'build heavy,'" explains award-winning production designer Alex McDowell.

But how to go about constructing a 1985 that never existed? Step one was a full immersion in the original work. "Everyone on my crew – the painters, the artists, the graphic designers, the prop masters – they've all taken a huge amount of time studying the graphic novel," says McDowell. "It's definitely a kind of mix of looking at real location references from the time, and then adding in this layer that the graphic novel frames."

One of the major locations heavily altered by construction crews was a recently abandoned Domtar paper mill, a site originally desired because its tremendous ceiling height was spacious enough to house Dr. Manhattan's lab and the incongruously lavish living quarters he shares with Laurie. The designers quickly appreciated that it could be used for Rorschach's prison as well. "We couldn't find a prison location in Vancouver with those familiar double-, triple-, quadruple-story stacked prison cells," explains McDowell. But because of a big slot in the concrete floor, they were able to construct two floors of physical prison cells – a little cramped, but with plenty of room for a decent riot – while relying on post-production to add the higher floors digitally.

Adrian Veidt's enormous fortress in the Antarctic wastes, Karnak, proved to be the largest set in the entire film. The main audience hall where the climactic fight occurs was fully constructed on a soundstage. It is a mix of '80s Modern and Ancient Egyptian monumental architecture, complete with a bank of forty television monitors. Views of the exterior and into adjoining passageways were accomplished via CGI.

But perhaps nowhere was this intensive approach to putting the graphic novel physically onscreen more fully realized than on the sprawling New York City sets that took shape on a former lumber yard outside of Vancouver, British Columbia. "This is really the hub of the *Watchmen* world... It centers around 43rd Street and 6th Avenue... Very seedy, very down... but with our own *Watchmen* overtone,"

McDowell explains. "There's nothing here that's background or generic. Everything is directly related to the story."

This New York City consists of three streets intersecting, each representing different parts of the city. In the north, Brownstone Street runs east to west. Here, Dan Dreiberg tinkers away in his upscale digs and dreams of his glory days. (Right across the street is the Saigon Bar, where the Comedian shoots the mother of his unborn child on VVN Day.) At the corner we stop at the newsstand where the two Bernies stand an eternal watch. Heading south along Porno Street, the garish facades of the burlesque houses and peep show parlors contrast with the rundown tenements across the street – one of which is where Moloch ends his days. A darkened alley yawns to our right, tempting us with the entrance to an illegal club or perhaps to a bull session with Hollis Mason in the rooms over his garage, but Knot Tops prowl nearby. Moving on, we reach the financial and fine dining center of Blake Street, also called Riot Street, for here Nite Owl and the Comedian descend in the Owlship to quell the populace during the Police Strikes of '77; it is also where the Comedian takes his final bow in '85.

Devotees of the graphic novel will be hard pressed, even on repeated viewings, to find any landmarks, signage, or even graffiti scrawls that have been left out from the source material. Recalling a visit to the set, artist Dave Gibbons writes, "At the corner, a Treasure Island store promises a bounty of pulp thrills; down the block, the Gunga Diner beckons, fully fitted out in chrome and purple leather and, over there, the Rumrunner sign looms luridly. Even the austere façade of the Institute For Extraspatial Studies can't spoil the gaudy fun… Detail piles on dizzying detail."

Watchmen, however, is not simply about creating a time that never was – it's about reflecting on a time that could have been. This required constructing a setting that was not only faithful to the vision of the graphic novel, but also convincing to the uninitiated. "It's really important for us to establish a world that is real to an audience," says McDowell. Crucial to obtaining the desired realism was weathering the exteriors to give the city that "lived-in" look. "Building by building," McDowell explains, "you go through and you build a layer, let it sit, let it age, let the rain hit it for a little while, then come back and do another layer… Every layer just makes it closer and closer to the vision."

Previous spread: Rorschach investigates Blake's apartment.

This spread: Dan visits his old friend and mentor, Hollis Mason.

This spread: Rorschach discovers Blake's inner sanctum.

Next spread: The renewable energy reactor in Dr. Manhattan's lab at the Rockefeller Institute.

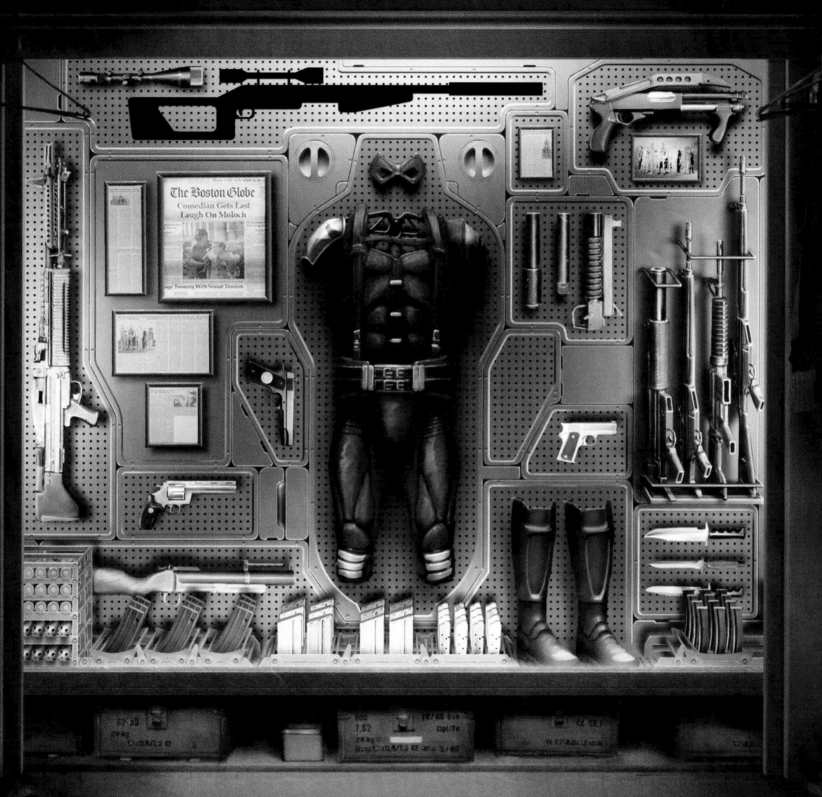

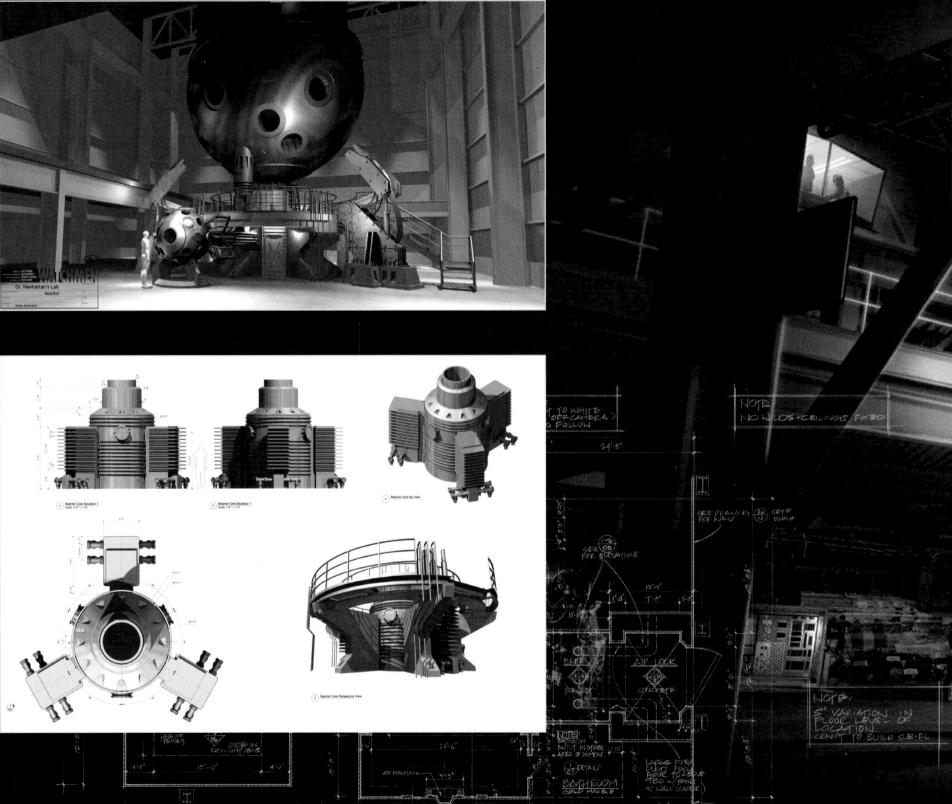

Dr. Manhattan, alone in his apartment at Rockefeller now that Laurie has left him, gets ready for his television interview.

Adrian Veidt's office mixes
the ancient with the ultra
modern.

Left: (Left to right): Director Zack Snyder, producer Deborah Snyder, and production designer Alex McDowell inspect a model of the New York set.

Opposite: The exterior of Moloch's apartment.

Previous spread: New York sprouted from a lumberyard in British Columbia.

This spread: The infinite layers of the *Watchmen* world. **Next spread:** The seedier, the better.

Signs of the times from the New York set, including the Gunga Diner and Hollis Mason's repair shop.

Above: Electric vehicles appear on the streets of the alternate New York, thanks to Veidt's technology.
Below: Two designs for the Electric Car Charger.

LEFT/ RIGHT SIDES   FRONT & BACK

15 3/4"

4"   6"

2x (2units)= x4 total   2x (2units)= x4 total

Paint:
-print x4 each on good vehicle wrap vinyl & di-cut
-apply to 2x units
-aging TBD

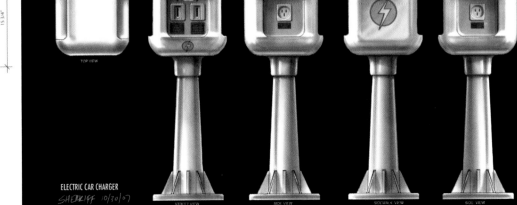

TOP VIEW

ELECTRIC CAR CHARGER
SHERRIFF 10/30/07

STREET VIEW   SIDE VIEW   SIDEWALK VIEW   SIDE VIEW

This spread: Early concept design for the Great Hall at Karnak.

Next spread: Another view of the Great Hall.

MY NAME IS OZYMANDIAS,
KING OF KINGS:
LOOK ON MY WORKS,
YE MIGHTY, AND DESPAIR!

Details of Veidt's home away from home, including a quotation from Shelley.

Above and below: The interior of Karnak's glass pyramid ceiling gets digitized.

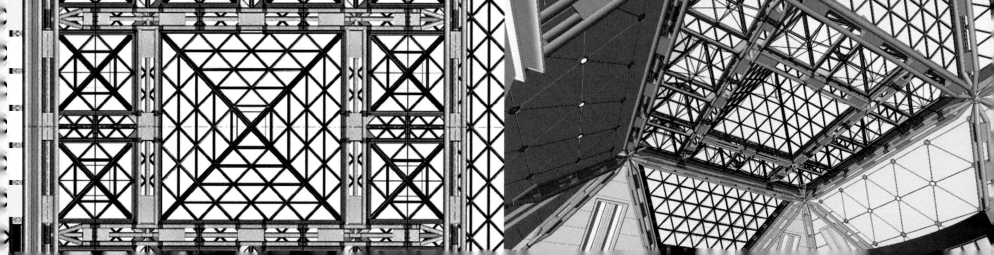

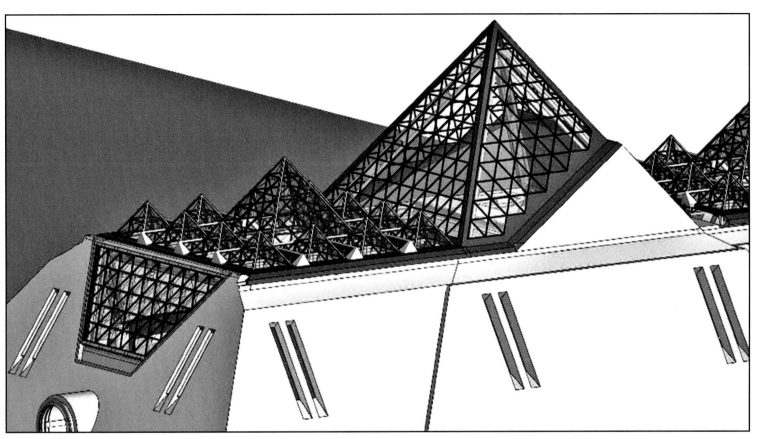

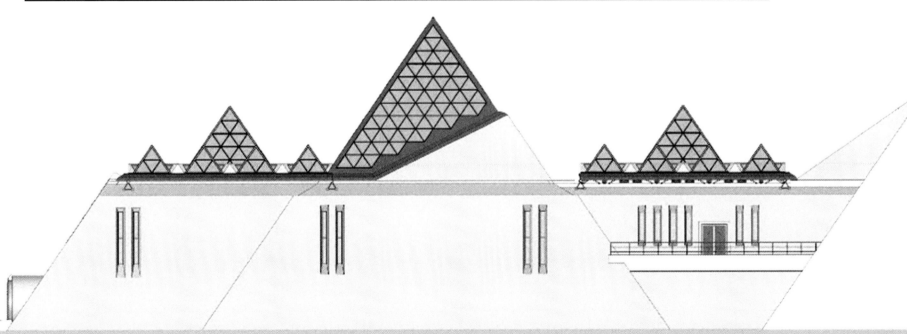

Archie comes in for a hard landing near Karnak.

PROPS

However well-built the sets, they need to be furnished, and that means more than just couches. Photographs and other mementoes need to be produced and placed in the scene. The right sorts of cars need to be customized and rolled in. Shop signage and advertisements need to be fabricated and hung. The most interesting prop, says property master Jimmy Chow, is one that not only blends in, but one "that adds to the story or adds to the character."

Watchmen, more than most productions, required a razor-sharp attention to detail when dressing a set. "The characters are very clearly defined and separated," explains production designer Alex McDowell. "We had to do the same with the environments, whether it's the color palette, or the props and set dressings surrounding them. Everything about their context and history, we've tried to build in... So, you can get all of the clues really embedded in every space."

The very first character and environment the audience encounters is Edward Blake, AKA The Comedian, relaxing in his high-rise apartment. Although we will grow to know him better after flashbacks throughout the film spanning his nearly fifty-year career, "It's the one time that you get to see what Blake would be like in his civilian guise," explains production designer Alex McDowell. Blake is a "...violent, sexual character, and we

compress that into his glitzy bachelor pad designed to bring women back to – full of ethnic sex toys from all over the place, herbs, and sex aids… He doesn't have much taste, and it's very glittery and ostentatious."

Adrian Veidt, on the other hand (who calls his alter ego Ozymandias, after the Greek name for Rameses II), sees himself as an heir to the philosopher kings of old, setting out to restore the ancient glories of the pharaohs and Alexander the Great. His Antarctic refuge of Karnak is part laboratory, part bunker, and part museum. "We thought in terms of him buying out the Cairo museum and taking these enormous artifacts by helicopter to Antarctica," says McDowell. Artisans recreated everything from giant sculptures down to friezes, weapons, armor, serving dishes, and jewelry to adorn his home away from home.

Veidt's office in his headquarters building also contains many ancient artifacts, but most of the dressing served to demonstrate the vast commercial reach of Veidt Enterprises. There are display cases full of Veidt Air jetliner models, bottles of Nostalgia perfume, and of course superhero action figures from the Ozymandias line. There is even a model of the building itself prominently on exhibit.

As well as helping define characters, the set dressing and props in the temporally schizophrenic *Watchmen* also provide visual cues as to the year and location depicted in each scene. "We have acres of research for each sequence, particularly all these flashback sequences, which are just three, four, five second shots, but they have to pinpoint the period… I think the story needs that to create the believability of what's going on presently," explains set decorator Jim Ericson. Rather

than use voiceovers and superimposing dates on the screen, "…we have created over twenty-eight newspapers of different time periods," says Chow. "Frames, columns, and all of those things – the newspapers are completely accurate, so the camera can go right into certain things and the picture can tell where we are."

Ericson admits to having reservations about the project before he was familiar with the graphic novel. "When I was talking to Alex (McDowell) before I started the picture, I said, 'You know, if you want someone to do fantasy, I'm not your person. My specialty is doing something real and doing something honest.' And he says, 'No, that's where we're going, that's what we wanna do.'" He says that only when filming was about to commence did it all click for him. "I got it. Suddenly it all made sense," he continues. "Zack was really quite adamant that things feel real, and to strike that balance between a comic book panel and reality… It's a strange kind of mix that I've never really encountered before."

One place where set dressing broke from canon was the choice of vehicles. Rather than the bubble-like electric cars of the graphic novel, the film features older models from the '70s and '60s for 1985 New York. The reasons for the change were largely story-based. "You don't have that many new cars," explains McDowell, "especially in the context of an imminent nuclear attack, where you're not gonna buy a new car." About a third of these received new paint jobs to fit the *Watchman* palette. Using older cars throughout also provided a contrast with the hopeful vibe of the rebuilt New York at the end of the film, when electric cars finally do make an appearance.

Opposite top: Confiscated weapons on display at Minutemen Headquarters.
Opposite bottom left: Spaceman's raygun.
Opposite bottom right: The Comedian's pistols, presented to "Edward Blake with gratitude" by the Nixon administration.

Above: Design for Nite Owl II's laser pistol.

A sampling of Nite Owl
II's gadgetry.

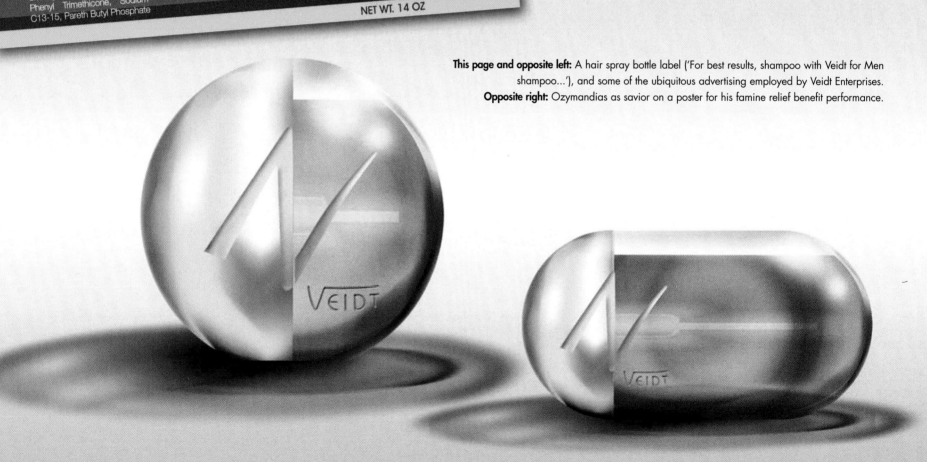

VEIDT
FOR MEN

DIRECTIONS: For best results, shampoo hair with VEIDT For Men Shampoo followed by VEIDT For Men Conditioner. Hold can 12-16 inches away from hair. Spray in an even, all around motion to hold style overall. Repeat spray on areas where maximum hold is desired.

CAUTION
EXTREMELY FLAMMABLE

CAUTION EXTRTEMELY FLAMMABLE. PRESSURISED CONTAINER. KEEP AWAY FROM SUNLIGHT AND DO NOT EXPOSE TO HIGH TEMPERATURES. DO NOT SPRAY ON OR AROUND A NAKED FLAME. KEEP AWAY FROM SOURCES OF IGNITION DURING USE AND UNTIL HAIR IS FULLY DRY. INTENTIONAL MISUSE BY DELIBER-ATELY CONCENTRATING AND INHALING CONTENTS CAN BE HARM-FUL OR FATAL. USE ONLY IN A WELL VENTILATED ROOM. AVOID EYE CONTACT. IF THIS OCCURS, RINSE THOROUGHLY WITH WATER. KEEP OUT OF THE REACH OF CHILDREN. DO NOT PIERCE CANISTER. USE ONLY AS DIRECTED.

INGREDIENTS: Alcohol 40-B, Dimethyl Ethyl, Water, Ethyl Ester of PVM/MA Copolymer, Amin-omethyl Propanol, Fragrance, Phenyl Trimethicone, Sodium C13-15, Pareth Butyl Phosphate

VEIDT
FOR MEN

HAIR SPRAY
FOR MEN

Super Hold

NET WT. 14 OZ

Nostalgia

VEIDT
ENTERPRISES

This page and opposite left: A hair spray bottle label ('For best results, shampoo with Veidt for Men shampoo...'), and some of the ubiquitous advertising employed by Veidt Enterprises.
Opposite right: Ozymandias as savior on a poster for his famine relief benefit performance.

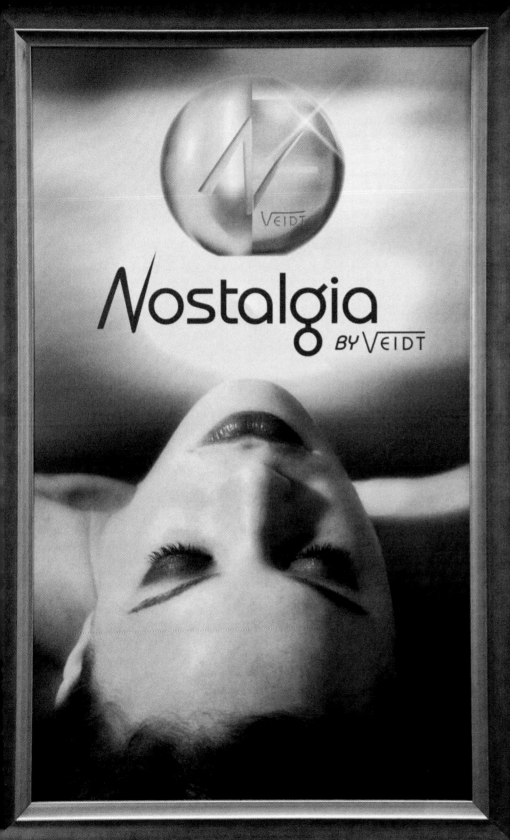

Clockwise from above: A homemade Hooded Justice doll; the remains of Blaire Roche; a clipping from *The New York Gazette* about the capture of Rorschach.

WALTER KOVACS
62186

WALTER KOVACS
62186

During A
Wanted
By WILLIAM BALL
Special to The New York Gazette

NEW YORK - Walter Joseph Kovacs, also known as Rorschach, was arrested last night when a squadron of police officers led by Detectives Fine and Bourquin, surrounded the house of Edgar William Jacobi, following an anonymous tip.

Kovacs, who was on the premises at the time, injured two police officers while resisting arrest. Officers Shaw was admitted to the hospital with minor burns, while Officer Greaves, who was shot at point blank range with a gas-powered grappling gun, has a shattered sternum and is still on the hospital's critical list as of this writing.

When the house was explored, the body of Edgar Jacobi was discovered in the kitchen, shot through the head. The murder weapon was found less than two feet away, and although there were no fingerprints on the gun it should be remembered that since Kovacs was wearing gloves when arrested, this lack of prints is hardly remarkable. Although Kovacs has denied the murder of Jacobi, given his previous history of violence against other criminals and his location in the murder house

Above: Helo pilot's helmet from 'Nam. **Left:** The prop cleaver Rorschach "buried" in the child murderer's skull.

BY
HOLLIS
MASON
A.K.A. NITE OWL

AN AUTOBIOGRAPHY
UNDER THE HOOD

New York Fire Department
In Appreciation of
Many Years of Association
presented to
"The Nite Owl"

NEW YORK CITY
FIRE DEPARTMENT
In Gratitude of
"THE MINUTEMEN"
for Assistance With
Civic Emergencies
June 15, 1951

MEMB...
FIGHT ...

MINUTEMEN
1940

The New York Gazette.

FINAL

MYSTERIOUS MASKED
MAN CLEANS UP WHARF

MURDEROUS
RAMPAGE
AVERTED

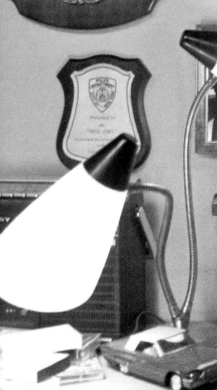

The New York Gazette

FINAL

U.S. SENDS
DIPLOMATS
TO HANOI

HERO RETIRES

Writes Tell All Book

UNDER THE HOOD

Detroit Cars

Previous spread: Hollis Mason (Nite Owl I)'s tell-all biography and his wall of accolades.

This page above and right: Nite Owl I's costume, preserved for posterity.

Opposite: Several copies of Hollis Mason's retirement statuette.

WE FIX 'EM!

OBSOLETE MODELS A SPECIALTY

2'-7"

5'-0"

CLOSED

WE FIX 'EM!

OBSOLETE MODELS A SPECIALTY

FINAL
★★★★★

The New York Gazette.

WEATHER

VOL. LXXXIX No. 29,898   NEW YORK, FRIDAY, SEPTEMBER 15, 1938   THREE CENTS

MYSTERIOUS MASKED MAN CLEANS UP WHARF

WEST MILFORD

'Nite Owl' leads suspect to authorities.

THE UNITED STATES OF AMERICA

TO ALL WHO SHALL SEE THESE PRESENT GREETINGS:

THIS IS TO CERTIFY THAT
THE PRESIDENT OF THE UNITED STATES OF AMERICA
AUTHORIZED BY ACT OF CONGRESS MARCH 3, 1863
HAS AWARDED IN THE NAME OF THE CONGRESS TO

'MINUTEMEN'

THE MEDAL OF HONOR

FOR

CONSPICIOUS GALLANTRY AND INTREPIDITY INVOLVING
RISK OF LIFE ABOVE AND BEYOND THE CALL OF DUTY
IN ACTION WITH THE ENEMY

Masked Vigilantism, New York City, NY in the year of Nineteen Hundred and Thirty-Six

GIVEN UNDER MY HAND IN THE CITY OF WASHINGTON
THIS TWENTY SEVENTH DAY OF MARCH 1936.

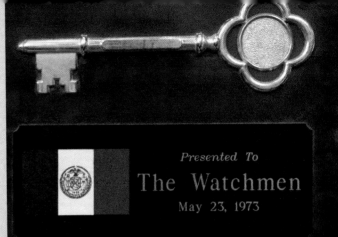

Presented To
The Watchmen
May 23, 1973

NEW YORK CITY
FIRE DEPARTMENT
In Gratitude of
"THE MINUTEMEN"
for Assistance With
Civic Emergencies
June 15, 1951

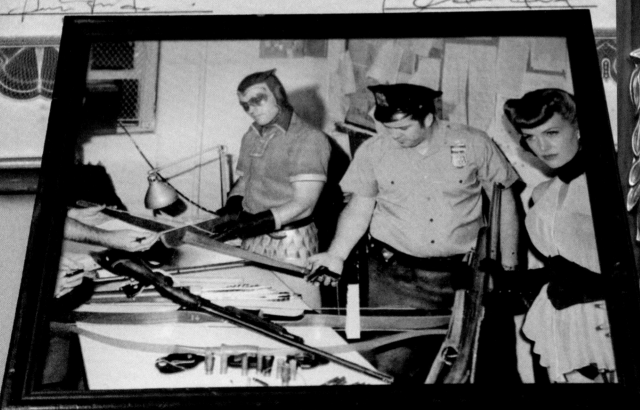

Previous spread: Hollis Mason's crime-fighting memorabilia (and repair shop sign).

Opposite: Sally Jupiter (Silk Spectre I)'s collection of happy memories from her glory days.
Above and right: A "Tijuana Bible" and a treasured snow-globe.

This spread: Ozymandias's meticulous map does not impress the Comedian.

Next two spreads: A few of the many period newspapers created for the film.

NEW FRONTIERSMAN

★★★★

50 cents

HONOR IS LIKE THE HAWK: SOMETIMES IT MUST GO HOODED

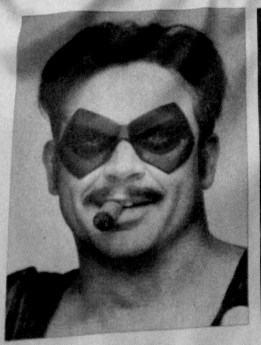

Hector Godfrey, Editor

RED ARMAGEDDON!

Would our sense of national identity, our pride, our sense of honor; ...on the ... things be so enduring were it not for such great symbols ... Alamo, or the

DOOMSDAY CLOCK AT 5 TO MIDNIGHT

Scientists Fear Imminent Nuclear Threat

By M. J. GEISTHARDT
Special to The New York Gazette

WASHINGTON - Not since 1953 has the Doomsday Clock been so close to midnight. The clock is now at 5 Minutes to Midnight asserts The Bulletin of the Atomic Scientists. The clock conveys how close humanity is to catastrophic destruction--the figurative midnight--and monitors the means humankind could use to obliterate itself with war and nuclear weapons.

The Bulletin of Atomic Scientists blame the growing tensions between the USA and the USSR in the last four years for what it seems will likely be the end of humankind.

After a period of relative stability in 1972, when the clock was at 12 Minutes to Midnight due to the Strategic Arms Limitation Treaty (SALT) and the Anti-Ballistic Missile (ABM) Treaty, designed by the United States and Soviet Union in an attempt to curb the race for nuclear superiority, the state of the world's safety has continued to steadily decline.

Now, since 1981, the clock arm has fluctuated dangerously close to midnight between 5 minutes and 2 minutes. 1981 saw the clock tick to 4 Minutes To Midnight because the Soviets invaded Afghanistan, causing Americans to stiffen. The US pulled out of the Moscow Olympics in a

clear message that the US would not tolerate the Soviet invasion activities. Nixon also decided that the best way to win the Cold War was to finally win it. Since then he has been steadfast at trying to do so while promoting peace. Critics see this as the main reason Americans and the rest of the world do not trust him more than they do the Soviets.

Last year the the clock was at 3 Minutes to Midnight. Dialogue between the two superpowers virtually stopped. In their Bulletin, the Atomic Scientists reported, "Every channel of communications has been constricted or shut down; every form of contact has been attenuated or cut off. And arms control negotiations have been reduced to a species of propaganda". Then the US began doing research into developing or purchasing a space-based anti-ballistic missile capability. The US was highly criticized for completely ignoring arms control agreements made in previous years. The world over, people had been concerned that a new arms would ensue.

Now Nixon has made a symbolic effort to discuss peace and amicable relations with the Soviets. He has just returned from Geneva where he met with Soviet Premier Gorbachev. Not much was accomplished. Gorbachev and his foreign minister demanded to know more about the US's intentions for Dr. Manhattan. Nixon refused to divulge any information regarding Dr. Manhattan, the atomically altered scientist who has fought for the US in previous wars.

Nixon refused to divulge any information regarding the mutant

The Watchdog Group of Nuclear Scientists has reset the Doomsday Clock.

continues to work as a scientist".

US Foreign Analyst, Professor Blake William PhD. is concerned that this Geneva talk has done more harm than good, "Our President called the summit promising peace talks and giving the illusion of transparency. However, I believe his refusal to discuss what the rest of the world thinks is the most pressing topic,

Premier Gorbachev made his comments regarding his dissatisfaction with the summit, leading many in the US to believe that the summit did more harm than

Continued on Page Two, Column 5

Geneva Talks, U.S. Refuses to Discuss Dr. Manhattan

By WILLIAM BALL
Special to The New York Gazette

GENEVA, SWITZERLAND - President Nixon and Soviet Premier Mikhail Gorbachev met in Geneva for three days this week to talk about peace, international diplomatic relations and the arms race. President Nixon called the meeting in response to the tense atmosphere between the two superpowers and the ticking metaphorical Doomsday Clock, which is reportedly at 5 minutes to midnight.

In their meeting, Gorbachev and his foreign minister demanded to know more about the US's intentions for Dr. Manhattan, or what the soviets call "the Unfair Advantage" or "The Living Weapon". Nixon refused to divulge any information regarding Dr. Manhattan, the atomically altered scientist who has fought for the US in previous wars. He only said, "Dr. Manhattan is a scientist and continues to work as a scientist".

After the summit, Gorbachev said in a comment to the press, "We viewed the Geneva meeting realistically, without grand expectations, yet we hoped to lay the foundations for a serious

President Nixon is unwilling to discuss, what the world knows to be, the biggest threat to the safety and future of the planet, should it go unchecked, then the roots for a serious problem grow".

US Foreign Analyst, Professor Blake William PhD. is concerned that this Geneva talk has done more harm than good, "Our President called the summit promising peace talks and giving the illusion of transparency. However, I believe his refusal to discuss what the rest of the world thinks is the most pressing topic, shows that we are hiding something".

It still seems to early to tell what effect the summit has had on the Soviet leaders. While Americans wait, The White House has declined offers to release a comment with their review of the summit.

William worries that the longer The White House declines comment, the more fear and unrest will show up on the streets in America. Americans need answers too. Poor leadership creates mistrust and revolt.

It was former president Eisenhower who championed the great need for world leaders to have personal relationships in order to

Continued on Page Two, Column 5

BUSCH TARPAULIN TRAPS CARDS'

BELGIAN PREMIER

SOVIETS CALL DR. M. 'IMPERIALIST WEAPON'

President Nixon Responds with Public Statement

By ALLEN WYNDER
Special to The New York Gazette

WASHINGTON - President Nixon has responded to the Soviet slander, which called our Dr. Manhattan an imperialist weapon last week, with a televised public statement. The statement denounces the Soviet claims, defends Dr. Manhattan's actions and calls Russian foreign policy the perfect example of Imperialism.

President Nixon said, "Dr. Manhattan only has peace in mind. He was a physics scientist through and through and has the interests of the betterment of the world through peace and science in mind. The fact that he has superhuman powers only amplifies the need for him to do his part because he has the ability."

The soviets specifically called for Dr. Manhattan to leave Vietnam saying that "the Americans are not fighting a war but simply taking over a country with extreme force". Additionally, they accused Dr. Manhattan as being just one aspect of a multi-tiered imperialist plan, with oil sales and control and armament sales to weak nations as being the other aspects.

It is true that next to Manhattan science and oil, armaments is one of the most profitable industries worldwide. Selling arms to the countries of Asia, keeps the U.S. war industry operating. It continues a

thieving, corrupt core of the military monopoly, which is the main monopoly support base for ultra-right and fascist movements, both here in the U.S. and world-wide.

President Nixon also said, "Dr. Manhattan is not part of any plan. He operates of his own free will according to his values as an American and as a scientist." In response to the armaments sales accusations, the President had no comment other than to say, "The USA has various alliances with different countries. Just as it has for years. Just like the rest of the world has. To divulge our ally secrets would be silly."

The Pentagon and Arms Dealers are Pushing this Secrecy Policy

Locksmith and McDonald Dennahead, along with the Pentagon and arms dealers, are pushing this secrecy policy. What they won't tell you though is that the weapons sales to countries surrounding Vitenam are related to the policy of exploitation and imperialism's profits - more guns, more profits.

Russia also claimed that Dr. Manhattan's force and the armament campaign in South Asia, also serve to keep German, British and French imperialism out of South and Central Asia. U.S. corporations view other countries as competitors. But not all countries of Asia will be able to get U.S. arms

choice will be picked by the U.S. corporations that have property in these countries. The arms will be sold to countries where U.S. corporations have the largest holdings.

The arms will be sold to countries with the most reactionary governments. U.S. imperialism wants to arm the countries that can be used in the aggression against North Vietnam. U.S. imperialism will sell arms to countries that will use them against their own working class.

The President Reassures the American People

Our President closed by reassuring the American people that, "whatever the Soviets say or think, is

Continued on Page Two, Column 5

NARCOTICS EDUCATION PROGRAM NOW

Drug Use Amongst Teens Rises at Alarming Rate

By DOUGLAS GARDNER
Special to The New York Gazette

A drug education program for high schools

Dr. Manhattan has been listed as a threat to Soviets.

Soviet Foreign Minister Andrei Gromyko declares that his government is very upset over US domination, declaring Dr. Manhattan as a secret weapon. Diplomatic channels have cooled between the super powers. The White House has yet to respond.

Senator Refutes Claims of Money Mismanagement

By VERONICA LEWIS
Special to The New York Gazette

NEW YORK - Senator Charles Goodell is refuting claims that his department has been squandering money on frivolous things since his expenditures have become public.

over the top," he described. But the senator's office is not just spending money on food. They are mismanaging money on social projects and campaigning aswell. Ever since his 1967 campaign for office, the Goodell camp

Some people insisted that this same board be loaned bond money to bail the district out. How could anyone have confidence enough to make these mismanages a loan? If the district were a private business it could not

RUSSIA DEMANDS WORLD INQUIRY

Soviets Ask for Investigation Into Origins of Dr. M.

By E. J. HORNIG
Special to The New York Gazette

MOSCOW — General Secretary of the Communist Party of the Soviet Union Leonid Brezhnev demanded Friday to a government investigation of the Origins of Dr. Manhattan in 1959, less than a week after he reportedly dismissed the idea by saying it might turn into "a political show."

The move by Putin seeks to place criticism on the US after he had earlier ruled out a public probe of the super man's origins, saying that Russia didn't have the money to pursue the matter. Russian officials have also repeatedly cast the military campaign in Chechnya as part of a war against international terrorism.

U.S. Defense Secretary, Larry Beaver, said Friday that it the US didn't have to divulge anything they didn't want to. "I mean, why should we tell you. Maybe if we had a vested interest in doing

FAMILY OF SIX KILLED IN HOME FIRE

Two Children Away, Now Orphaned

RORSCHACH REVEALED

Daring Arrest Nabs Wanted Murderer

By WILLIAM BALL
Special to The New York Gazette

NEW YORK - Walter Joseph Kovacs, also known as Rorschach, was arrested last night when a squadron of police officers led by Detectives Fine and Bourquin, surrounded the house of Edgar William Jacobi, following an anonymous tip.

Kovacs, who was on the premises at the time, injured two police officers while resisting arrest. Officers Shaw was admitted to the hospital with minor burns, while Officer Greaves, who was shot at point blank range with a gas-powered grappling gun, has a shattered sternum and is still on the hospital's critical list as of this writing.

When the house was explored, the body of Edgar Jacobi was discovered in the kitchen, shot through the head. The murder weapon was found less than two feet away, and although there were no fingerprints on the gun it should be remembered that since Kovacs was wearing gloves when arrested, this lack of prints is hardly remarkable. Although Kovacs has denied the murder of Jacobi, given his previous history of violence against other criminals and his location in the murder house at the time, few other conclusions seem possible.

Curiously, Kovacs has not denied the two other murders attributed to him, those of Gerald Anthony Grice, unemployed, in the summer of 1975, and of wanted multiple rapist Harvey Charles Furniss two years later in the summer of 1977, immediately following the passage of the Keene Act into law.

At the point of his arrest, the contents of Kovacs' pockets were as follows: 1 battery powered flashlight; 5 individually wrapped cubes 'Sweet Chariot' chewing sugar; a map New York underground and subway system, dated 1968 with recent alterations drawn in with a red ballpoint pen; withered remains of one red rose; one dollar fifty-nine cents in assorted loose change; one notebook, pages filled with what is either an elaborate cypher or handwriting too cramped and eccentric to be legible; one broken bottle 'Nostalgia' cologne for men, possibly broken during leap from Jacobi's second story window during arrest; a residue of ground black pepper.

Walter Joseph Kovacs, also known as Rorschach, was arrested last night when a squadron of police officers led by Detectives Fine and Bourquin, surrounded the house of Edgar William Jacobi, following an anonymous tip. Kovacs, who was on the premises at the time, injured two police officers while resisting arrest. Officers Shaw was admitted to the hospital with minor burns, while Officer Greaves, who was shot at point blank range with a gas-powered grappling gun, has a shattered sternum and is still on the hospital's critical list as of this writing.

When the house was explored, the body of Edgar Jacobi was

Continued on Page Two, Column 5

BODY FOUND AT SCENE OF ARREST

Edgar Jacobi A.K.A. Moloch Found Shot Dead

By M. J. GEISTHARDT
Special to The New York Gazette

NEW YORK - The body of Edgar Jacobi was discovered in his home during the apprehension of wanted criminal Joseph Kovacs, also known as Rorschach. Jacobi was shot through the head.

Walter Joseph Kovacs was arrested last night when a squadron of police officers who surrounded the house of Jacobi, following an anonymous tip. Kovacs, who was on the premises at the time, injured two police officers while resisting arrest.

When the house was explored, the body of Edgar Jacobi was discovered in the kitchen, shot through the head. The murder weapon was found less than two feet away, and although there were no fingerprints on the gun. Police believe that this is due to Kovacs' wearing gloves.

Although Kovacs has denied the murder of Jacobi, given his previous history of violence against other criminals and his location in the murder house at the time, few other conclusions seem possible.

Curiously, Kovacs has not denied the two other murders attributed to him, those of Gerald Anthony Grice, unemployed, in the summer of 1975, and of wanted multiple rapist Harvey Charles Furniss two years later in the summer of 1977, immediately following the passage of the Keene Act into law.

At the point of his arrest, the contents of Kovacs' pockets were as follows: 1 battery powered flashlight; 5 individually wrapped cubes 'Sweet Chariot' chewing sugar; a map New York underground and subway

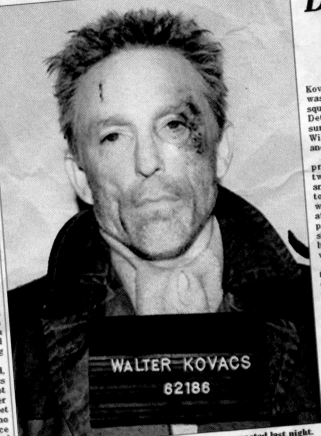

Walter Joseph Kovacs - A.K.A. Rorschach was arrested last night.

WALTER KOVACS
62186

LEADERS RESPOND TO SOVIET TROOP BUILD-UP

Firm Warnings from Western Leaders

By R. E. KLINGHOFFER
Special to The New York Gazette

WASHINGTON - The US and Britain had a quick response to the Soviet action taking place in Afghanistan. The White House called a Press Conference with President Nixon addressing the media on the question of military retaliation to the growing number of troops on the Afghanistan Pakistan border. The area know as the Frontier is a lawless stronghold of terrorism that cannot be tolerated. London backed President Nixon in his resolve to send troops to the region and urged the European powers to show the solidarity in dealing with the Russian government. Relations with Russia were further complicated when the Pakistan government denied that support was building among the military Generals who have influence on the Tribal Leaders of the region.

The US and Britain agreed that they would not make concessions to the Soviets but they were split badly over the question of punishment. The US is frustrated that the Soviets have escaped retribution in the past and are seeking firmer action in way of concessions. London was less insistent, perhaps because they have a much longer good term relationship with the Soviet Regime. Another issue is the fragile state of the Afghanistan economic problems as well as a persistent challenge from Muslim fundamentalists.

Trying to keep Nixon out of the fray, his aides made no changes to his public appearances and Nixon is due to speak to the Congress the following day.

Senior US intelligence sources confirmed that Soviet troop movement has been building for weeks with tanks amassed in the major areas around Kabul and the Khyber Pass.

The Kremlin is denying the report and has issued a statement denouncing any involvement in the affairs of the Afghanistan government.

St. Louis Readies for Kansas City Royals

By LEON BUCKLEY
Special to The New York Gazette

ST. LOUIS - The city is abuzz with activity as game three of the World Series is set for tonight. Pitting the two Missouri teams against one another, the '85 Fall Classic is known alternatively as the Show-Me Series and the I-70 Series. The Series opened in Kansas City, but St. Louis captured a taut 3-1 decision as the Royals missed a number of excellent scoring chances. The Cardinals won again the next night, scoring four times in the ninth inning after being shut out the previous eight. K.C.'s only two runs came in the fourth. The city is abuzz with activity as game three of the World Series is set for tonight.

World Series Game Three Tonight

Pitting the two Missouri teams against one another, the '85 Fall Classic is known alternatively as the Show-Me Series. I-70 Series and the Show-Me Series. The Series opened in Kansas City, but St. Louis captured a taut 3-1 decision as the Royals missed a number of excellent scoring chances. The Cardinals won again the next night, scoring four times in the ninth inning after being shut out the previous eight. K.C.'s only two runs came in the fourth. The city is abuzz with activity as game three of the World Series is set for tonight.

Pitting the two Missouri teams against one another, the '85 Fall Classic is known alternatively as the Show-Me Series. I-70 Series and the Show-Me Series. The Series opened in Kansas

Hijacked Plane Intercepted By USAF

By R. E. KLINGHOFER
Special to The New York Gazette

EGYPT - Four men representing the Palestine Liberation Front (PLF)

Opposite: Walter Joseph Kovacs is arrested. In other news, the Soviet troop build-up in Afghanistan continues.

Above: Rorschach's diary, open to show his last entry.

DOLLARS

rbe

TIME

OCTOBER 13, 1985

SUPE
Unite

ADR
VE

OZY
US
TO
TO

Aug. 26, 1985

NEW YO

THE

The
Economist

12 October 1985

New York City Decay

**What keeps
NYC bankers
up at night**

A survey after page 30

Business Hero

How Adrian Veidt redefined economic synergy

Drawing the line between fact and fiction becomes difficult when skimming the publications used as set dressing.

Priceless antiquities recreated for Adrian Veidt's office.

This spread: Egyptian gods share space with super-hero action figures from the Ozymandias line.

Next spread: Detailed views of the figures sculpted specifically for the film by artist Neville Page.

Opposite: Nite Owl II and Silk Spectre II immortalized in plastic.

Above: The Owlship as a highly marketable toy.

THE BLACK FREIGHTER

This and next spread: The *Black Freighter* comic, featuring the story "Marooned," is brought to life with a cover and splash page drawn by Dave Gibbons. The film's art department laid out the *Watchmen*-world-specific ads and the letters page.

COVER

SPLASH

GALLEY GOSSIP

SINCE LAST TIME...
A couple of things went wrong last month. My apologies to you all! First, I was so late with the Gally Gossip manuscript that a number of comics had to be printed without it! An ad was inserted in it's place. I'm sure you were all very worried!

Second, when the Gally Gossip was finally finished, it was already so late that I couldn't take the time to check it over properly before it went out. Therefore, the winning photos of last months ship contest was printed smaller than intended and looked muddy. This photo will be reprinted next month so all readers can see the one that took first prize.

MY REASONS ARE...
Last month I was on the road for nearly three and a half weeks, attending a spectacular convention in sunny southern California, and the incredible comic convention over on the east coast. Along with my regular travelling items, I took a large portfolio of work and my briefcase. However, I must admit that the sun and southern air had me giving in to temptation, and I ended up truly relaxing for the better part of a day. I played racquetball and lifted weights and the hotel's health spa. I went swimming in the hotel pool, body surfing at the beach, and partying far into the night. I was joined in these thoroughly childish activities by many fellow comic lovers who had made the journey to the convention. It was wonderful - the nearest thing I've had to a vacation in about five years.

WHAT'S BEING DONE...
Well, I've already arranged for many of your favorite pirate personalities to do guest columns which will appear on this page every once in a while when I think you buccaneers out there need a change of pace- or when I'm in a jam!

ON WITH NEW BUSINESS...
Did any of you out there not see the sixteen page guide to comic collecting which was included in every single copy of your favorite ship story, which will remain nameless? From the response we received, it's the most popular bonus feature ever offered in a comic book! If you somehow missed it, head for the comic specialty shop nearest you. Many of them ordered a bunch of extra copies, and they may still have a few left. If you don't know of any comic specialty shops near you, check the ads in this comic! Many shops and distributors advertise here. Or, write to me. I'll get back to you with a list of shops in your general area.

Speaking of such shops, I'd like to thank the Treasure Island comic emporium for there help and cooperation, without which we couldn't have published the collector's guide at all! They originated the guide, and did thousands of collectors across the country a service by allowing us to publish and widely distribute it. Thanks, folks!

I HAVE TO MENTION...
...That in California, our own Editorial Director was honored with a prestigious award, acknowledging his contribution to the comics industry.

If you want to see one reason why, buy or borrow a copy of The Black Freighter. It'll convince you! A bunch of our other folks have received honors as well over the years. I'll run a complete list on this page one day soon.

CONGRATULATIONS...
...Are in order for my former secretary Ed. I've mentioned and thanked him here many times before. Being my secretary has got to be the toughest job in the place. I don't try to make it that way- really I don't! It involves representing us here to the world and to the free lancers, handling an enormous workload including tons of memos, letters, complicated projects, all of them urgent and important, supervising three or more office assistants, and putting up with me. Ed took it all in stride- so well, in fact, that he received an impressive promotion. He's now Administrative Manager of International Licensing. Wow!...I feel like I shout salute just writing that title. Congratulations!

TIL' NEXT TIME...
Good luck with the booty hunting out there and don't forget about the treasure map contest. Submissions will be accepted until the end of next month.

CLASSIC PIRATE THRILLS!

DC

TALES OF THE BLACK FREIGHTER

307 DEC

75¢

NO! IT'S BEARING STRAIGHT DOWN ON ME!

IN THIS ISSUE: MAROONED!

FEINBERG

11/7/07 6:59:55 PM

Frames from the animated version of "Marooned." Snyder and screenwriter Alex Tse filled in the gaps and expanded the narrative of the comic book, while Reel FX of Dallas, Texas brought the story to life. Gerard Butler provided the voice of the ill-fated mariner. Released on DVD alongside the theatrical run of *Watchmen*, the atmospheric tale has also been fully integrated into an extended director's cut of the film.

THE OWLSHIP

Batman has his Batmobile, Wonder Woman has her invisible jet, and Nite Owl has his Owlship. Designed and built by aeronautical engineer and bird enthusiast Dan Dreiberg in the abandoned subway tunnel beneath his family brownstone, he refers to the machine affectionately as "Archie" (short for Archimedes, Merlin's owl in T. H. White's *The Once and Future King*). The flying submersible is such an integral part of the *Watchmen* story – both in helping Dan get his mojo back and transporting him and Rorschach to Karnak – it is almost a character in its own right.

"The Owlship is one of the icons of the novel. Everybody recognizes it," says production designer Alex McDowell. Despite the ship appearing in many places in the book, designers were left with considerable leeway as to how to translate it to the screen. McDowell admits it was "great fun to design, because you start with this simple form… But you could go either way when you look at the graphic novel: a very slick

kind of sci-fi craft, or something that really you believe could fly." As with the sets, the costumes, and just about everything else in *Watchmen*, believability won out. "One of the references for us in building this was military vehicles," continues McDowell. "Sort of a mixture of something that might go deep sea [diving], with a helicopter, with a Harrier jump jet – but also sort of Russian space race. Very functional, nothing very polished." Ultimately, it had to be a craft the audience could believe Dan built himself.

Luckily, Dan would have help from lead sculptor and former custom yacht builder Jack Gauvreau, who set about transforming artists' renderings and digitized blueprints into a full-sized, three-dimensional object. He used traditional boat-building techniques and materials – double-plank mahogany ribbing, plywood, and fiberglass – to construct Archie over a period of fifteen weeks; at any one time, twenty people – carpenters, metal fabricators, painters, electricians, etc. –

could be swarming over the ship, adding their touches.

"I guess the biggest challenge was to get this to do everything they wanted it to do. They want it to fly. They want it to be static on a gimbal. They want parts to wild off for camera access. So, the big challenge for me was to give them a full structural unit... And have it as light as possible," recalls Gauvreau. Extras included working lights and thrusters.

It would also have to be an extremely versatile craft, as this single ship would be serving as not only a prop and a vehicle, but also as a set. One of the design concerns was that the ship's size was such that it made it difficult to "cheat" in order to make filming interior scenes easier. "Very often you build, say, a larger [separate] interior than an exterior, but we decided we would find the right scale and build it as an interior/exterior piece," McDowell explains. "It's proved to be one of the most fun sets in the movie for us."

Fun or not, the cramped set proved challenging to the camera crew,

but director of photography Larry Fong – a long-time veteran of Zack Snyder film shoots – took it all in stride and knew the end result would be worth it. "Everything we've done in the Owlship, we've really done *in* there, despite the man-scent and heat in the room," he jokes. "We're doing dolly moves and stuff in there. It's crazy."

For shots of Archie soaring over New York City or crash landing in the Antarctic wastes, however, Snyder needed a CG version. A LiDAR system was used to laser scan the full-sized practical Owlship and translate these precise measurements into a 3-D model.

Like the New York City sets, Archie needed to look used. "It's covered in scratches and scrapes," says McDowell, describing a deliberate treatment to simulate a very functional and well-worn piece of crime fighting equipment. And it looks right at home roosting in the Owl Chamber, which, if you look very closely, sports a few bruises and missing bricks from Dan's early flight tests.

Previous spread: Archie circles the prison during the riot.

This spread: Concept for the Owlship crash landing in the Antarctic near Karnak.

187

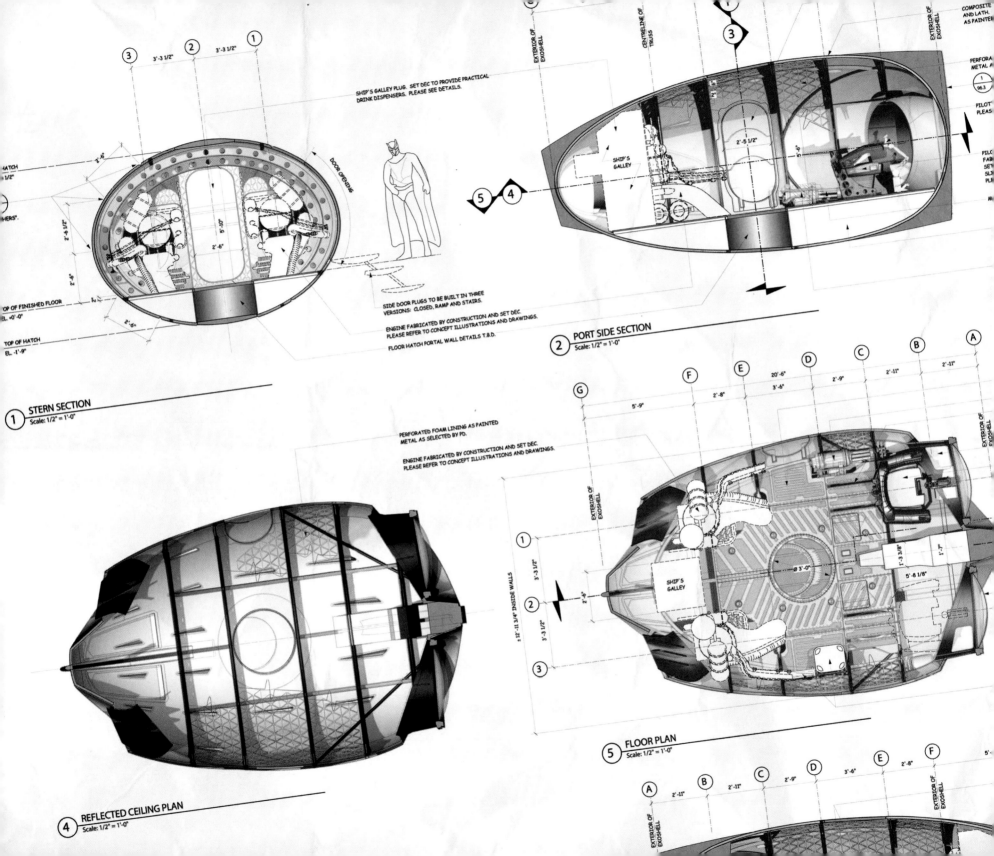

SHIP'S GALLEY PLUG. SET DEC TO PROVIDE PRACTICAL
DRINK DISPENSERS. PLEASE SEE DETAILS.

SIDE DOOR PLUGS TO BE BUILT IN THREE
VERSIONS: CLOSED, RAMP AND STAIRS.

ENGINE FABRICATED BY CONSTRUCTION AND SET DEC.
PLEASE REFER TO CONCEPT ILLUSTRATIONS AND DRAWINGS.

FLOOR HATCH PORTAL WALL DETAILS T.B.D.

DOOR OPENING

TOP OF FINISHED FLOOR
EL. +0'-0"

TOP OF HATCH
EL. -1'-9"

① STERN SECTION
Scale: 1/2" = 1'-0"

② PORT SIDE SECTION
Scale: 1/2" = 1'-0"

SHIP'S
GALLEY

PERFORATED FOAM LINING AS PAINTED
METAL AS SELECTED BY PD.

ENGINE FABRICATED BY CONSTRUCTION AND SET DEC.
PLEASE REFER TO CONCEPT ILLUSTRATIONS AND DRAWINGS.

SHIP'S
GALLEY

Ø 3'-0"

⑤ FLOOR PLAN
Scale: 1/2" = 1'-0"

④ REFLECTED CEILING PLAN
Scale: 1/2" = 1'-0"

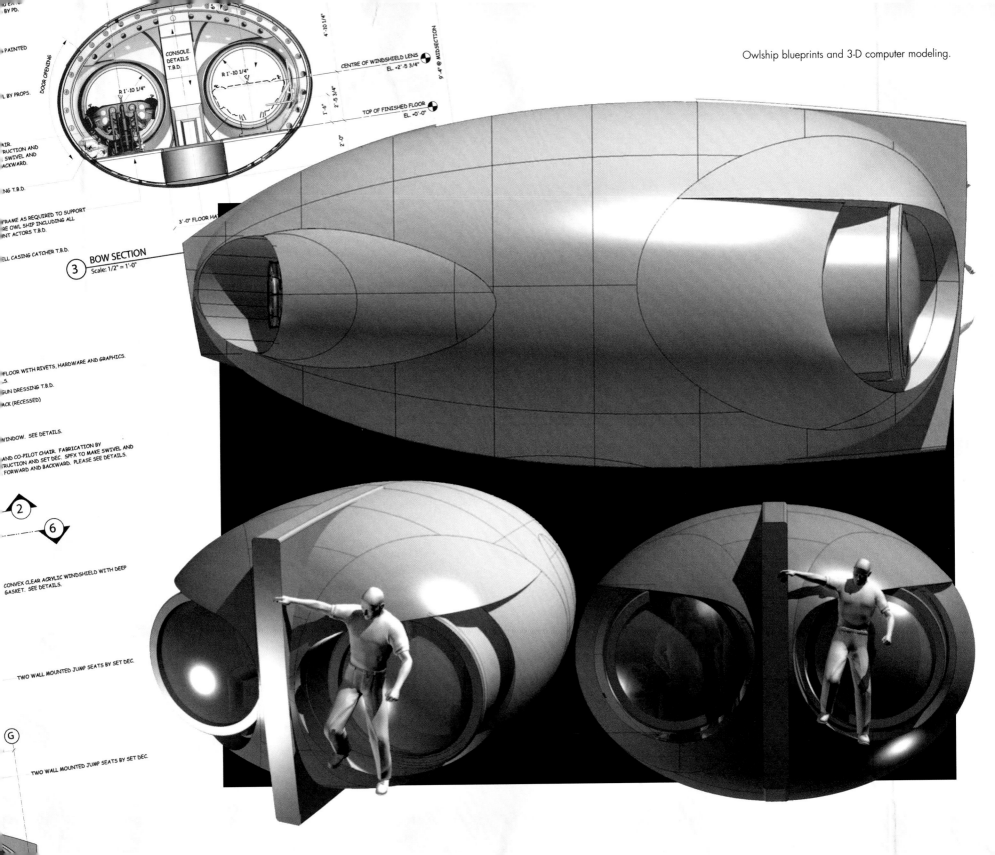

Owlship blueprints and 3-D computer modeling.

BY PD.

PAINTED

BY PROPS.

IR.
RUCTION AND
SWIVEL AND
ACKWARD.

NG T.B.D.

FRAME AS REQUIRED TO SUPPORT
RE OWL SHIP INCLUDING ALL
NT ACTORS T.B.D.

ELL CASING CATCHER T.B.D.

③ **BOW SECTION**
Scale: 1/2" = 1'-0"

FLOOR WITH RIVETS, HARDWARE AND GRAPHICS.
S.
GUN DRESSING T.B.D.
ACK (RECESSED)

WINDOW. SEE DETAILS.

AND CO-PILOT CHAIR. FABRICATION BY
RUCTION AND SET DEC. SPFX TO MAKE SWIVEL AND
FORWARD AND BACKWARD. PLEASE SEE DETAILS.

②

⑥

CONVEX CLEAR ACRYLIC WINDSHIELD WITH DEEP
GASKET. SEE DETAILS.

TWO WALL MOUNTED JUMP SEATS BY SET DEC.

Ⓖ

TWO WALL MOUNTED JUMP SEATS BY SET DEC.

CONSOLE
DETAILS
T.B.D.

DOOR OPENING

R 1'-10 1/4"

R 1'-10 1/4"

4'-10 1/4"

CENTRE OF WINDSHIELD LENS
EL +2'-5 3/4"

2'-5 3/4"

1'-6"

TOP OF FINISHED FLOOR
EL -0'-0"

2'-0"

9'-4" @ MIDSECTION

3'-0" FLOOR HA

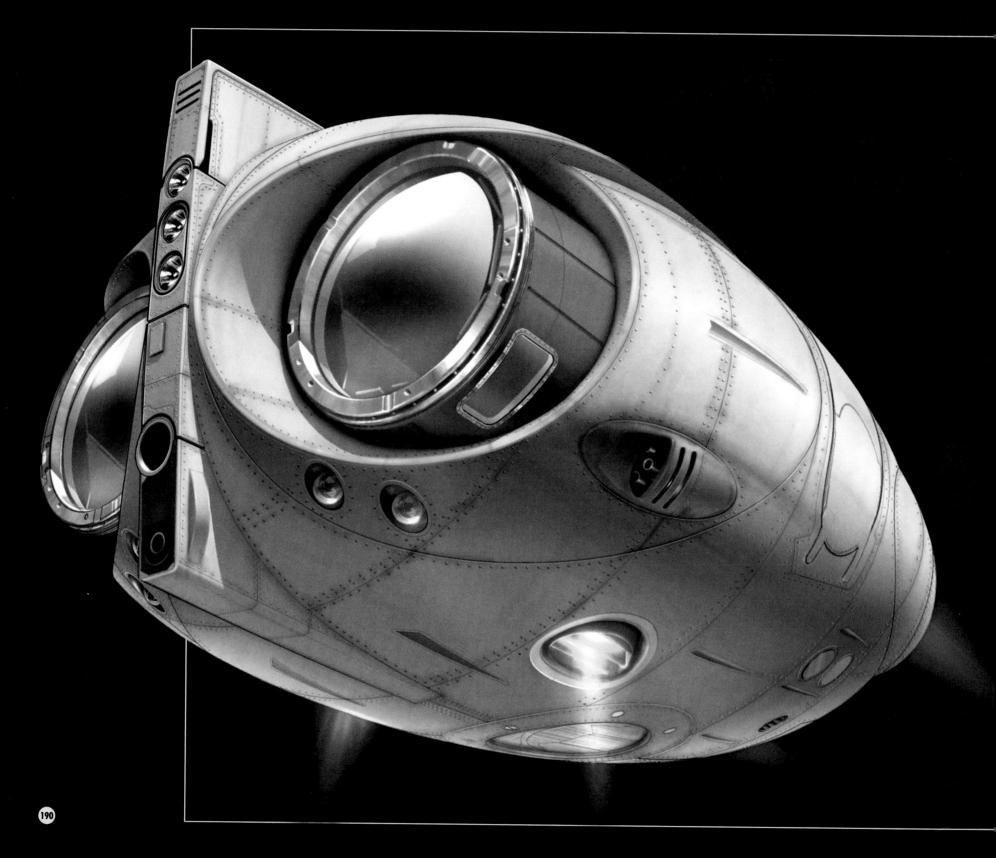

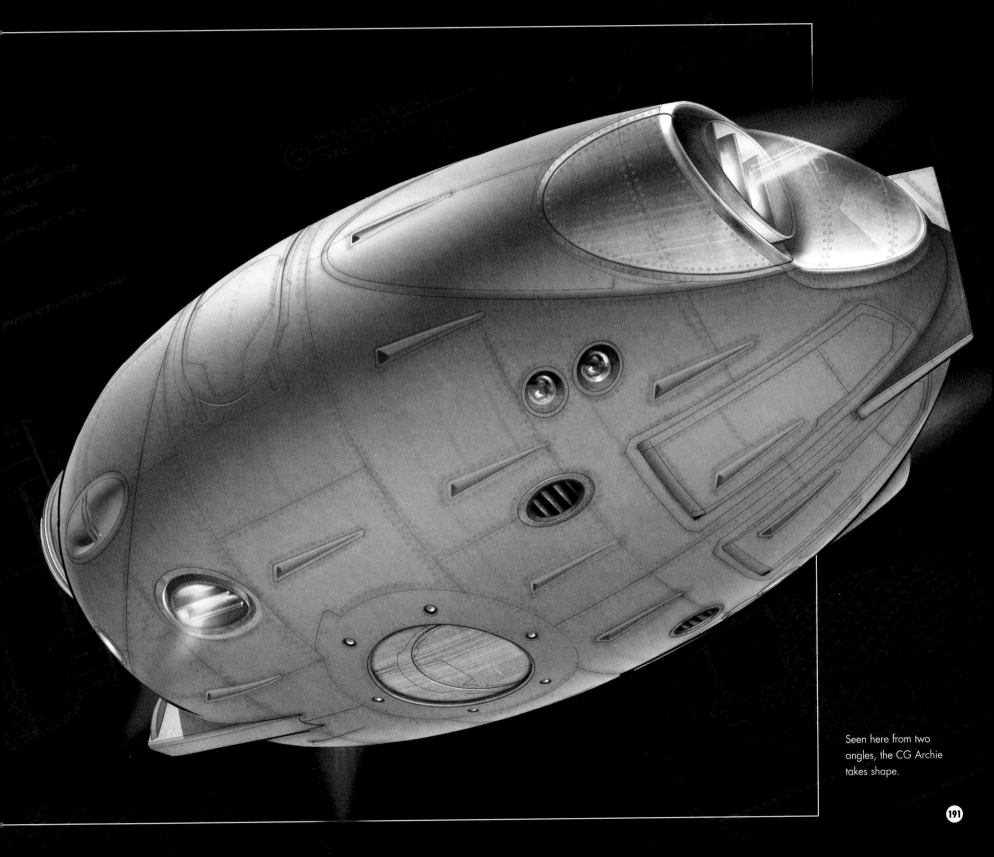

Seen here from two angles, the CG Archie takes shape.

Above and right: Details of access hatch and gun ports.

Opposite: Close-up of control surfaces.

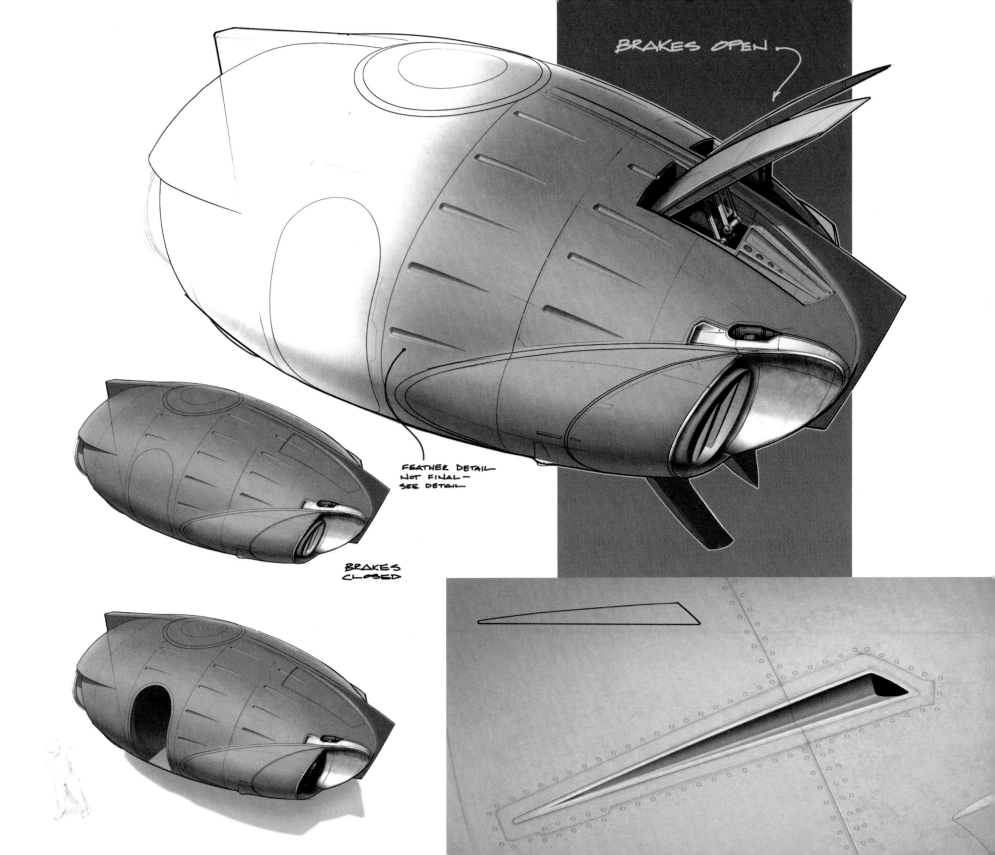

BRAKES OPEN

FEATHER DETAIL
NOT FINAL —
SEE DETAIL

BRAKES
CLOSED

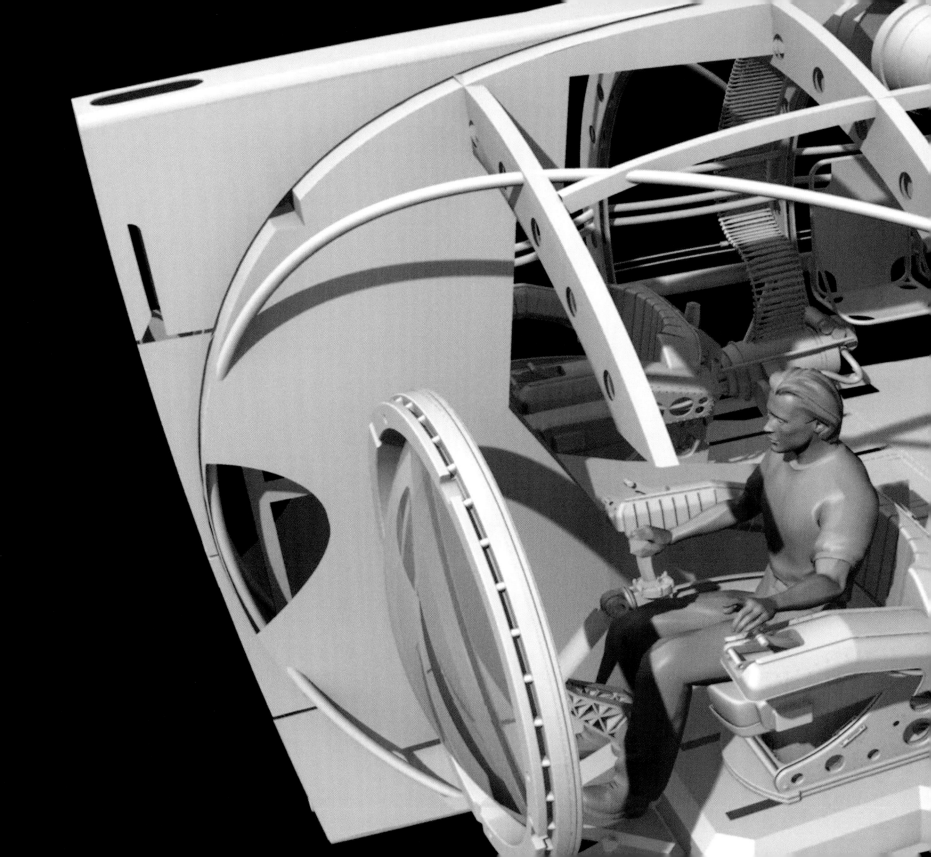

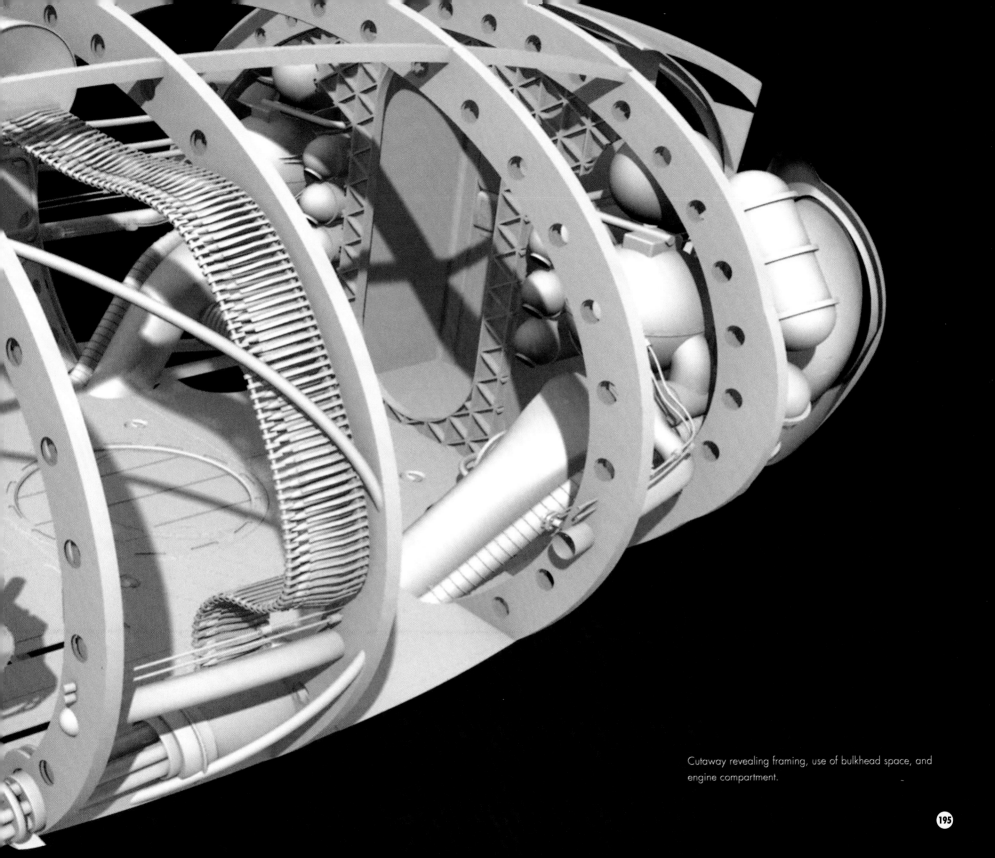

Cutaway revealing framing, use of bulkhead space, and engine compartment.

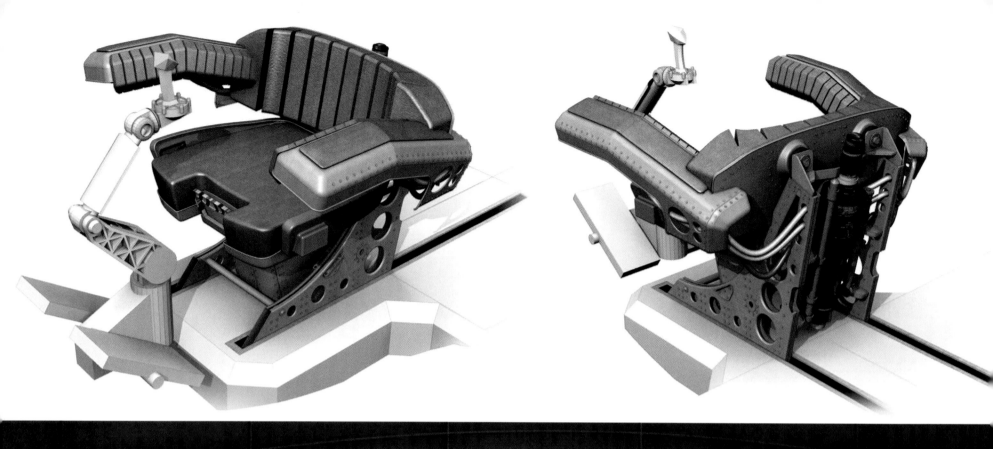

Above: Detailed rendering of the pilot's seat and control stick. **Below:** Plans for constructing the pilot's seat.

Opposite above: Plans for the cradle gantry on which Archie rests in the Owl Chamber. **Opposite below:** Three views of the controller Dan uses to remotely pilot Archie.

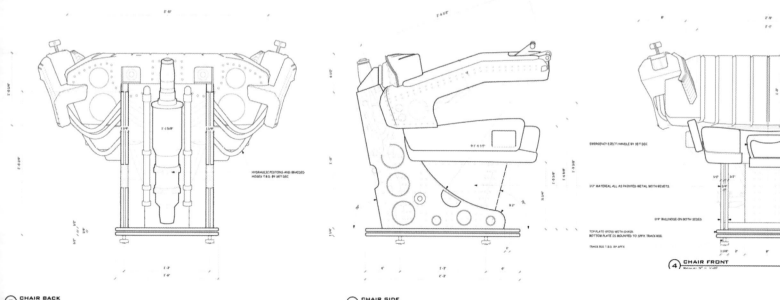

HYDRAULIC PISTONS AND BRAIDED
HOSES T.B.D. BY SET DEC.

EMERGENCY EJECT HANDLE BY SET DEC.

1/2" MATERIAL ALL AS PAINTED METAL WITH RIVETS.

1/4" BULLNOSE ON BOTH SIDES

TOP PLATE SPINS WITH CHAIR.
BOTTOM PLATE IS MOUNTED TO SPFX TRACK RIG.

TRACK RIG T.B.D. BY SPFX.

② CHAIR BACK
SCALE: 3" = 1'-0"

③ CHAIR SIDE
SCALE: 3" = 1'-0"

④ CHAIR FRONT
SCALE: 3" = 1'-0"

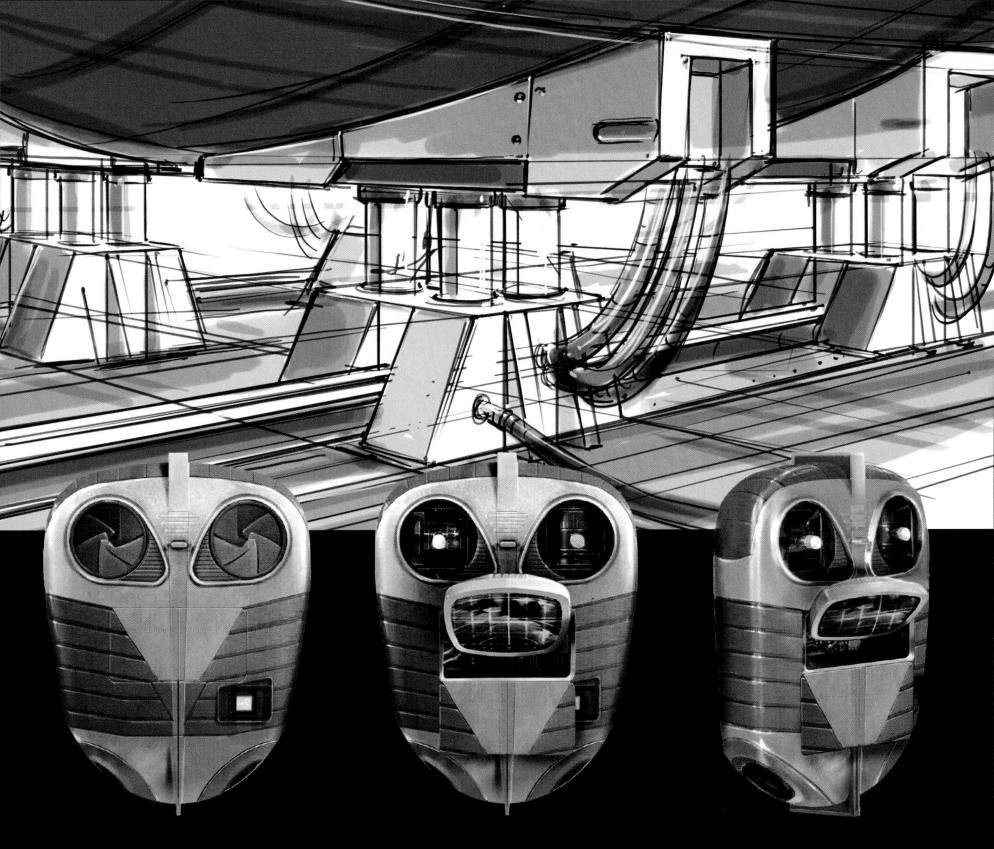

THE OWL CHAMBER

Left: Concept for the abandoned subway station that serves as the Owl Chamber.

Above: A graphic artist adds a detail to the Owlship's interior.

Above and below: The Owlship swoops in on the tenement fire. **Right:** CG sequence of Archie emerging from the East River.

Opposite: Concept of the Owlship roaring down the exit tunnel.

Below: Framing completed on the practical Owlship used for shooting.

Right: Status scans from the onboard monitors.

Opposite: Archie gathers dust in the Owl Chamber, waiting to be put back in action.

Award-winning costume designer Michael Wilkinson, who has dressed such films as *Garden State*, *Sky High*, *Babel*, and *300*, certainly had the résumé to tackle the comic book vs. reality dichotomy that *Watchmen* embodies. "We really tried to keep within the greens, the purples, the murky sort of secondary colors that are in the graphic novel," he explains, "but we also tried to pick beautiful, archetypical pieces that really summed up each decade and give a real sense of period authenticity to the movie." These included costumes for NYPD flatfoots circa 1940, '60s flower children, and Knot-Top punks of the '80s. "It was important to represent the 20th Century as it was, if there really had been super heroes."

Some of the costumes in the film could be seen as deconstructions and satires of costumes seen in super-hero movies of the past twenty years; this paralleled the tactic taken in the original graphic novel of referencing costumes from the Silver and Golden Ages of comic books. In whatever decade they inhabited, however, *Watchmen*'s super heroes needed to appear organic to the society that produced them. "We didn't want to feel like they were all rushed in from another universe. They were very much real to us," says Wilkinson. "We see the street clothes next to the super heroes – you can see that there's a link of humanity between." This influence of society was at least as important as characters' personalities when designing their costumes.

The Comedian, for example, is one of the original Minutemen. "We see him develop from a more naïve version in the 1930s, where he's getting his alter ego together. It's an old boiler suit that he's died green," explains Wilkinson. The Comedian's contemporaries, like Mothman, Hooded Justice, Dollar Bill, and the original Nite Owl, all sport a similar circus-performer aesthetic, wearing homemade costumes of traditional silks, leather, and woolen jersey fabric. By the '70s, however, the Comedian "becomes this armored tank of a character... Totally fortified with all of his weapons and his many strappings and layers of armor. He really hardens into this very nihilistic, world-weary, bitter character."

Rorschach is another character with a bleak outlook, but that doesn't stop him from trying to exact some justice from what is in his eyes an uncaring and unworthy world. Appropriately, he stopped caring about his own appearance long ago. Wilkinson points out, "He just wears this outfit, not to make a particular impression in the world, but just because it's what he wears. He keeps it in a dumpster. It has years and years of layers of crud and encrusted blood stains. And that's the whole litany of his past, read through his jacket." Getting Rorschach's mask right proved to be more challenging. "He doesn't really have any drapes or seams or anything like that. He just has this fantastic egg-head shape," recalls Wilkinson. "So we're creating a smoother piece to go under the final layer of fabric, so it erases all of the sharp details."

At the other end of the super-hero spectrum, Dan Dreiberg would have had considerably more money and scientific know-how when he designed his version of the Nite Owl II costume. "He has some resources to look into interesting materials that would be high tech in the late '60s and '70s," explains Wilkinson. There is a "feather-like" motif to his costume that might've been inspired by birds, but also it's a protective chainmail effect to his suit." Although the design was grounded in the graphic novel, "Zack wanted him to be a little awe-inspiring, a little fear-inspiring, when he walked down a dark alley," says Wilkinson. "When he puts the suit on, he's very powerful." Allowances were made for a corset, so Dan's midsection could be reined in during the height of his crime-fighting days of the '70s, and let out for post-retirement 1985.

Sally Jupiter and her daughter, Laurie – Silk Spectres I and II – have a love-hate relationship with each other and are very different women. Sally's revealing costume allowed her to use her exhibitionism as a tool in fighting crime. "She loved the attention. She was addicted to the idea of celebrity," says Wilkinson. Laurie's attitude towards vigilantism – and her costume – is much more ambivalent than her mother's. Laurie's costume has the same color scheme and silhouette as her mother's, "...but we rendered it in latex, 'cause we liked the idea of that extreme, hyper-sexualized version of her character, which juxtaposes so beautifully with Laurie's regular day-to-day character, who is very stitched together... She wants to be taken seriously," Wilkinson explains.

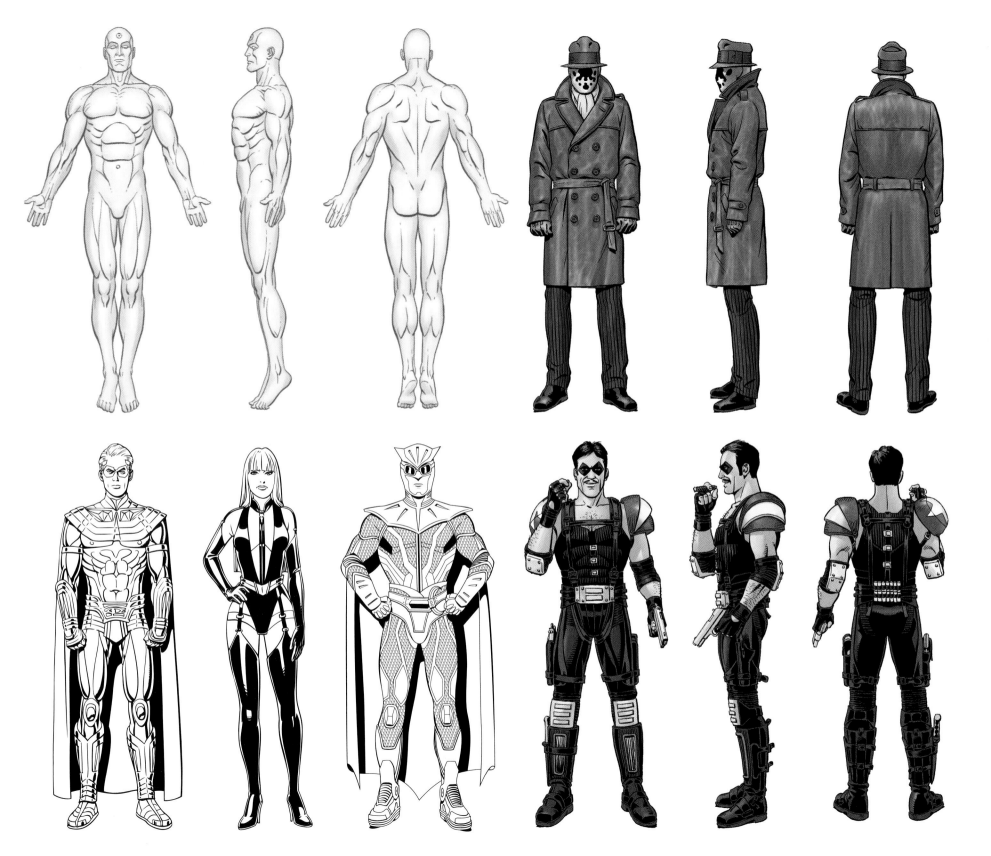

Sally Jupiter, AKA Silk Spectre I, goes from Dave Gibbons' original sketch (drawn in 1985 during the development of the original comic book series), through costume design, to fully fleshed out by actress Carla Gugino.

Villains from the Golden Age of costumed adventurers.
This spread: (Left to right) an unnamed villainess, Moloch the Mystic, Spaceman.

Next spread: Captain Axis meets Nite Owl I.

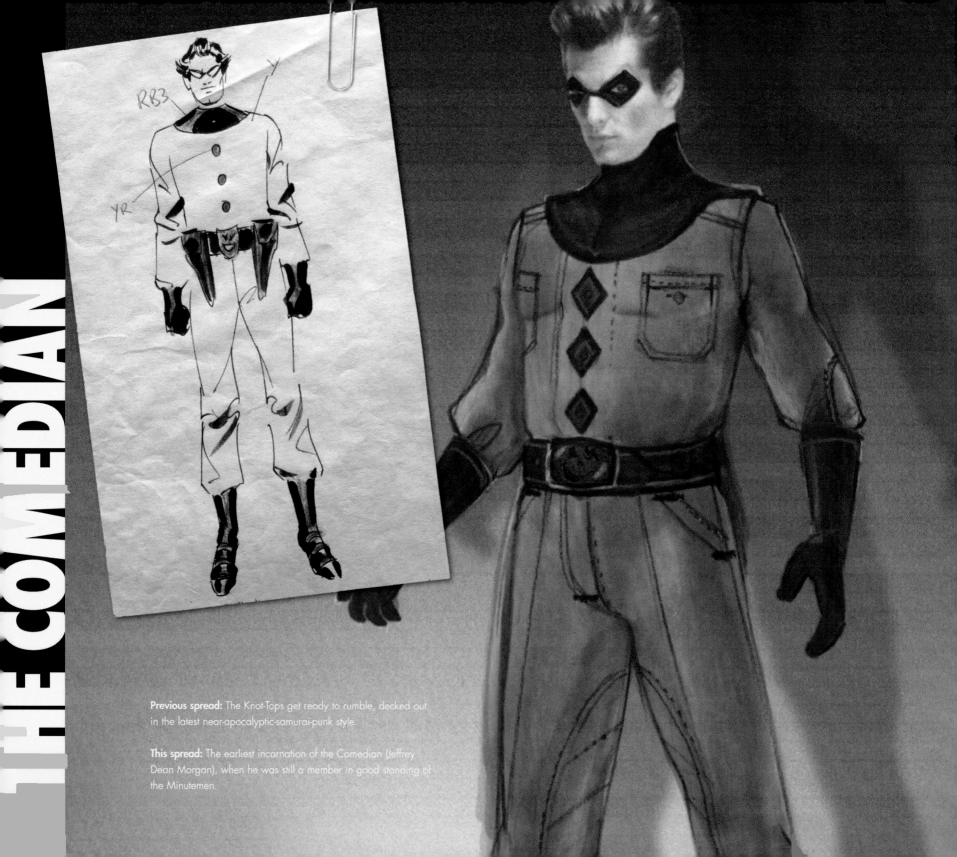

Previous spread: The Knot-Tops get ready to rumble, decked out in the latest near-apocalyptic-samurai-punk style.

This spread: The earliest incarnation of the Comedian (Jeffrey Dean Morgan), when he was still a member in good standing of the Minutemen.

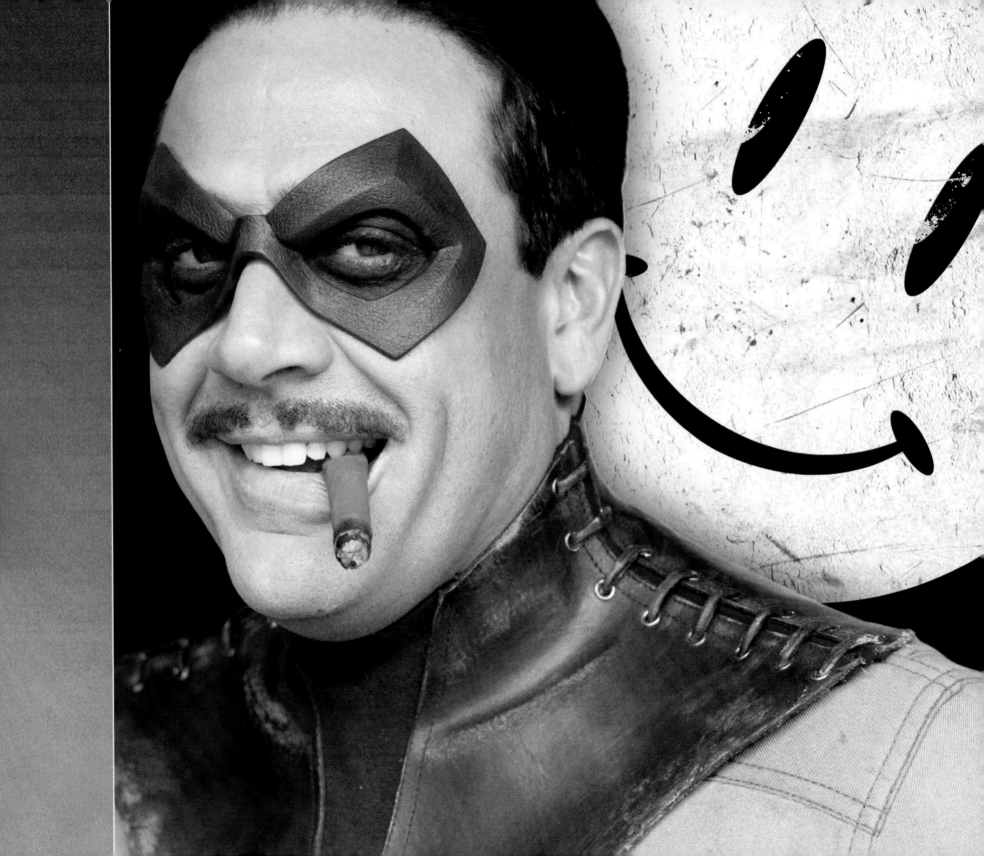

The Comedian changes with the times.
Left to right: Dressed for action in the South Pacific in WWII;
ready for a night on the town in the '60s; armored up for
Vietnam and covert ops in Latin America in the '70s.

Left to right: Dave Gibbons' 1985 concept sketch for Rorschach; final costume design; actor Jackie Earle Haley suited up.

Above and below: Original inkblots designed for the film, used to convey Rorschach's emotional states.

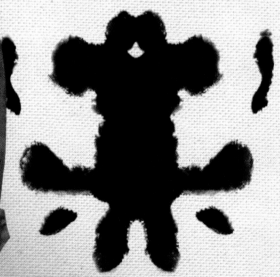
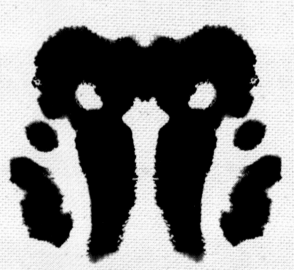

THE
END
IS
NIGH

Jackie Earle Haley as Walter Kovacs, AKA Rorschach, on the street and in the joint.

WALTER KOVACS
82186

This spread: Dr. Manhattan, AKA Jon Osterman, needs to be well-dressed both before and (albeit less often) after his horrific nuclear accident.

Next spread: Dr. Manhattan (Billy Crudup) meets President John F. Kennedy.

NITE OWL II

NITE OWL

Above and right: Nite Owl II makes the leap from comic book to cinematic deconstruction.

Opposite: Patrick Wilson embodies both Nite Owl II and Dan Dreiberg.

Details and concepts for Nite Owl II's costumes for use in extreme environments.

SILK SPECTRE II

This spread: Costumes for the many moods of Laurie Juspeczyk.

Opposite: Malin Akerman strikes a fighting stance as Silk Spectre II.

OZYMANDIAS

This spread: Called by some the smartest man in the world, Adrian Veidt will settle for the smartest dressed, whatever the occasion.

Opposite: Ozymandias (Matthew Goode) suited up to save the world.

POSTERS

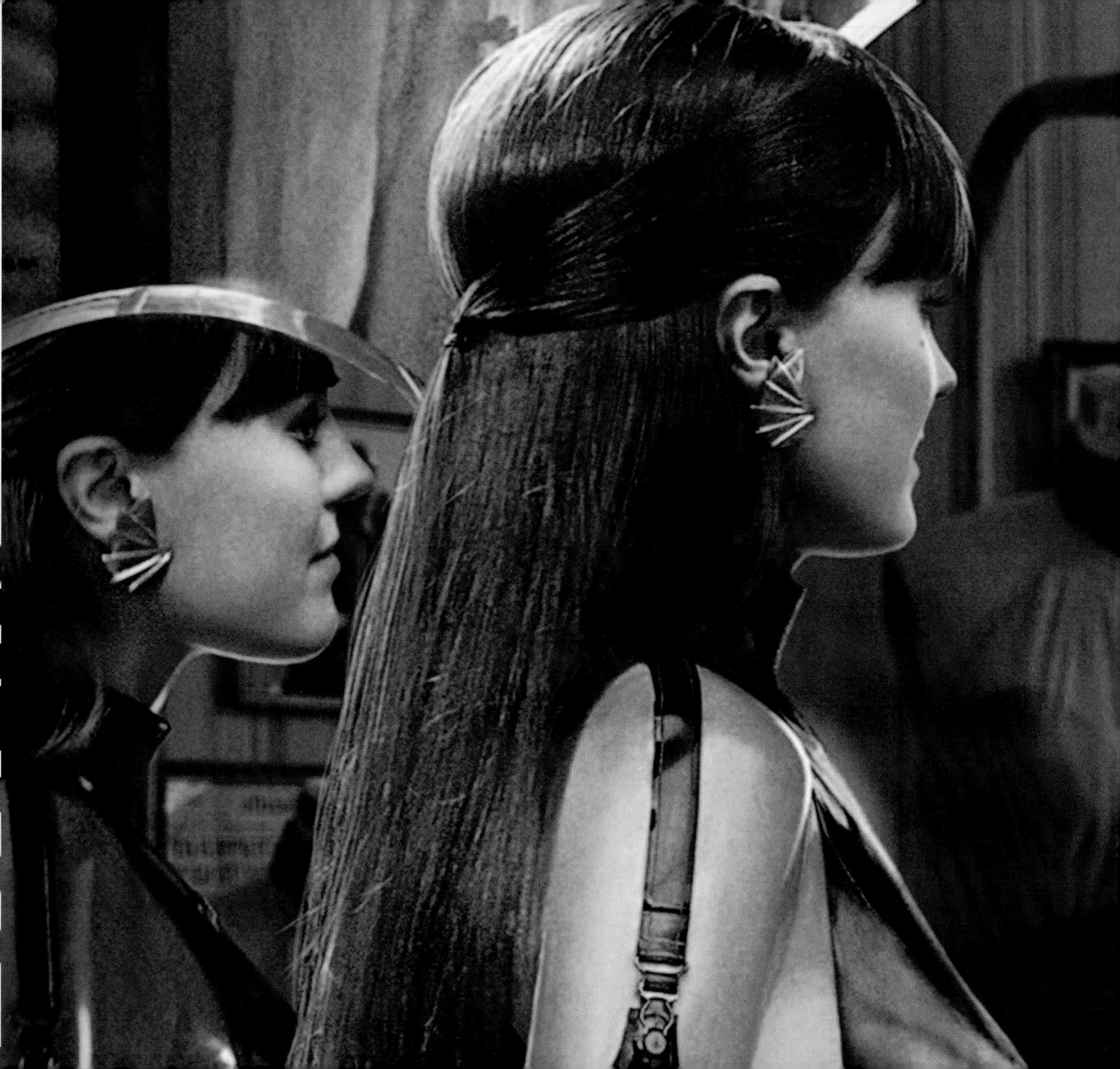

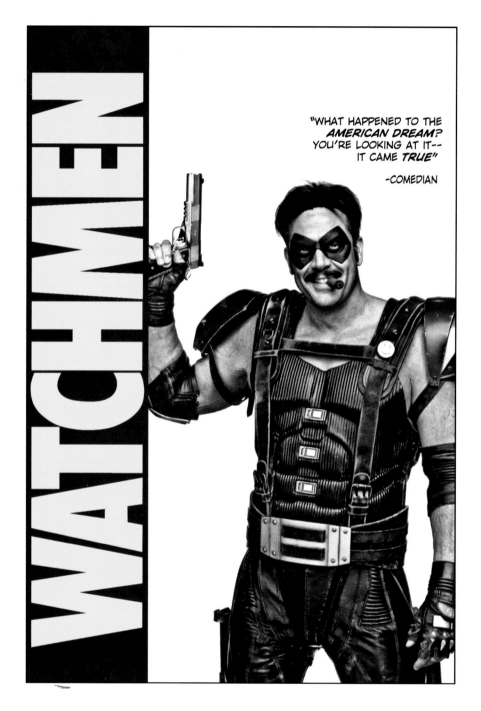

WATCHMEN

"WHAT HAPPENED TO THE *AMERICAN DREAM*? YOU'RE LOOKING AT IT-- IT CAME *TRUE*"

-COMEDIAN

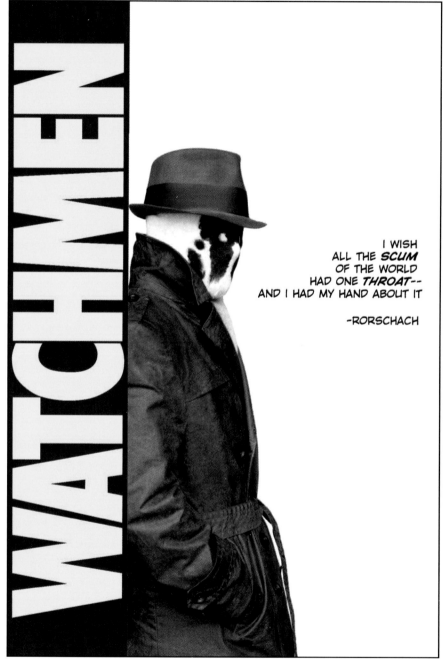

WATCHMEN

I WISH ALL THE *SCUM* OF THE WORLD HAD ONE *THROAT*-- AND I HAD MY HAND ABOUT IT

-RORSCHACH

This spread and next spread left: Unused mock-ups for deconstructed super-hero posters, featuring blank backgrounds, blunt quotes from each character, and lots of attitude.

WATCHMEN

"IT RAINS ON THE *JUST* AND THE *UNJUST* ALIKE... EXCEPT IN *CALIFORNIA*

-SILK SPECTRE

WATCHMEN

I'M USED TO GOING OUT AT *THREE IN THE MORNING* AND DOING SOMETHING *STUPID.*

-SILK SPECTRE

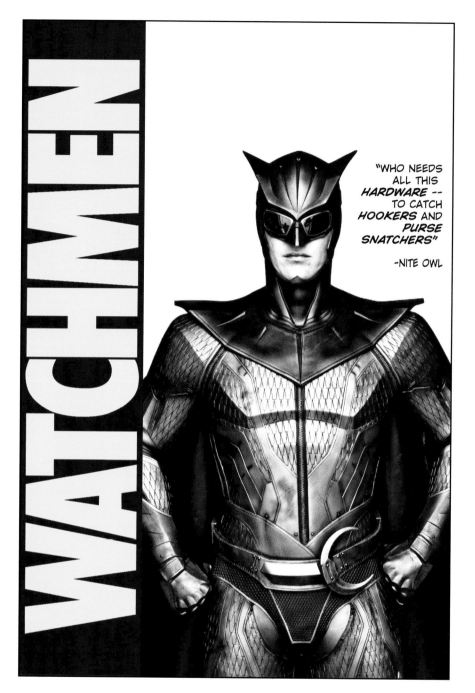

WATCHMEN

"WHO NEEDS ALL THIS *HARDWARE* -- TO CATCH *HOOKERS* AND *PURSE SNATCHERS*"

-NITE OWL

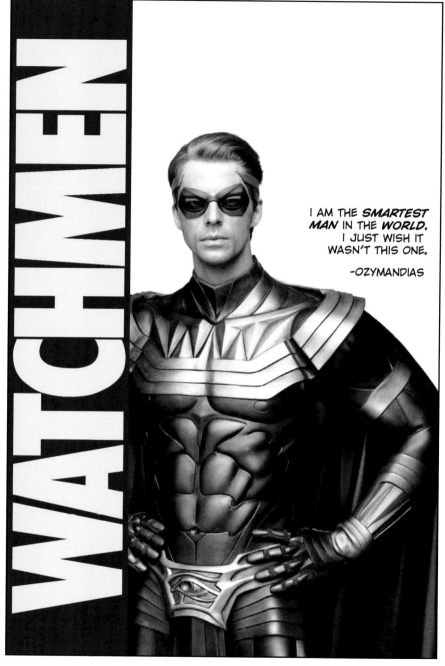

WATCHMEN

I AM THE *SMARTEST MAN* IN THE *WORLD*. I JUST WISH IT WASN'T THIS ONE.

-OZYMANDIAS

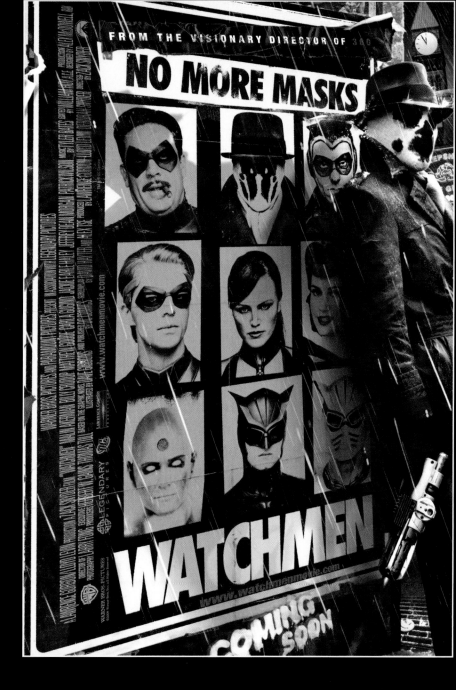

Above left: First poster announcing the film's release date, drawn by Dave Gibbons for Comic-Con 2007.

Above right: Rorschach won't be stopped, even by official threats, in this early concept for a one-sheet.

WATCHMEN

"It rains on the just and the unjust alike...
Except in California."

SALLY JUPITER, PALM SPRINGS (1985)

**FROM THE VISIONARY DIRECTOR OF '300'
BASED ON THE ACCLAIMED GRAPHIC NOVEL**

03.06.09

WWW.WATCHMENMOVIE.COM

This and next two spreads: Character-centered posters inspired by DC Comics house ads for the original *Watchmen* series.
Below: Dave Gibbons' early sketch for the Nite Owl house ad.

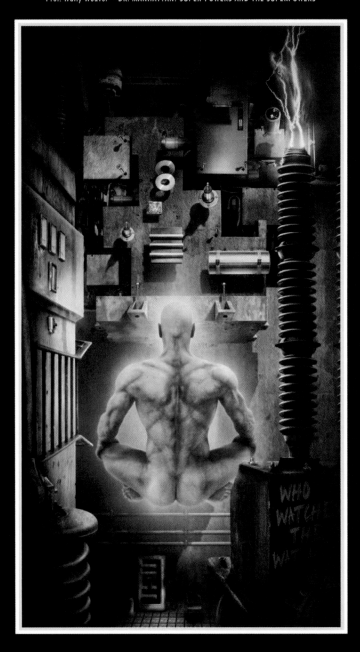

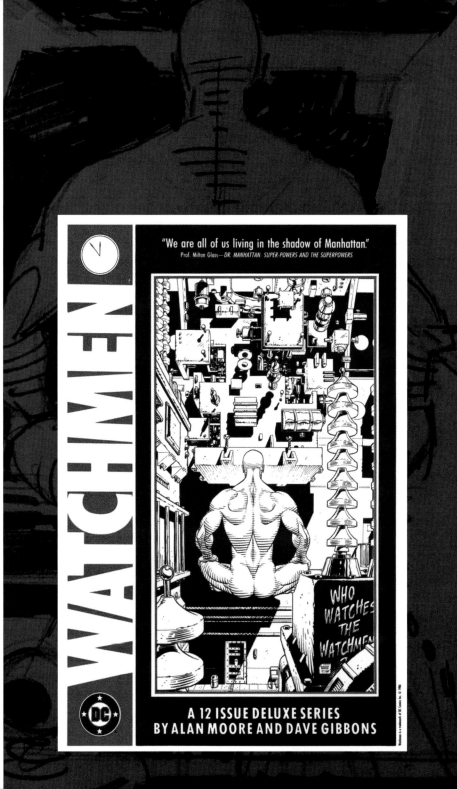

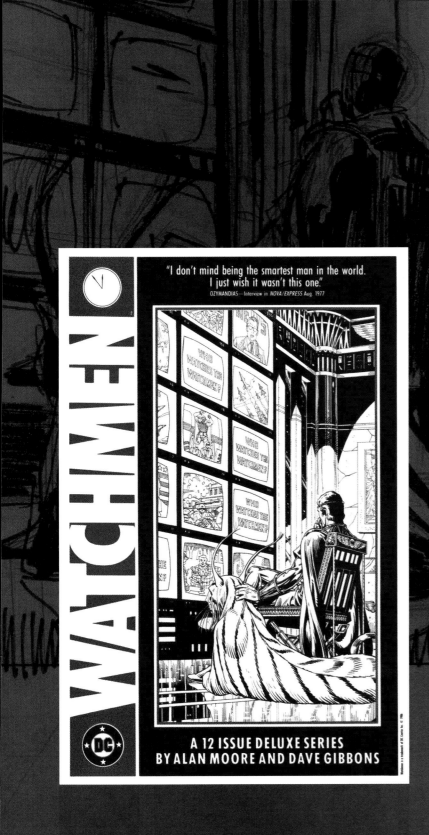

WATCHMEN

A 12 ISSUE DELUXE SERIES
BY ALAN MOORE AND DAVE GIBBONS

WATCHMEN

03.06.09

FROM THE VISIONARY DIRECTOR OF '300'
BASED ON THE ACCLAIMED GRAPHIC NOVEL

Above: Teaser posters from fall, 2008.
Next two spreads: The first character posters.

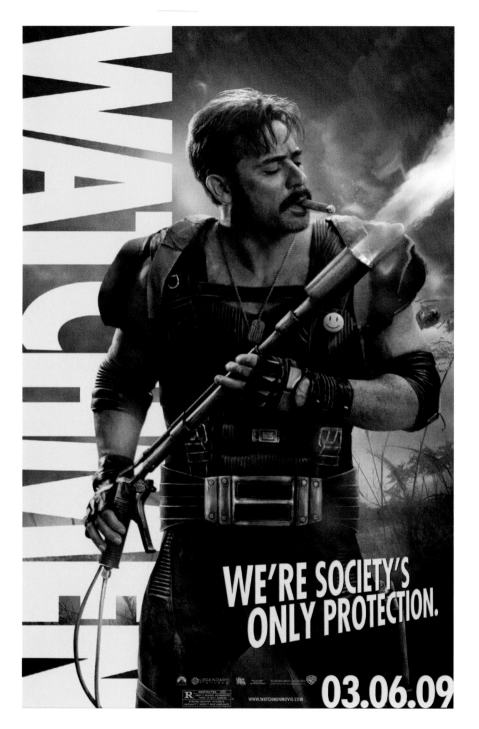

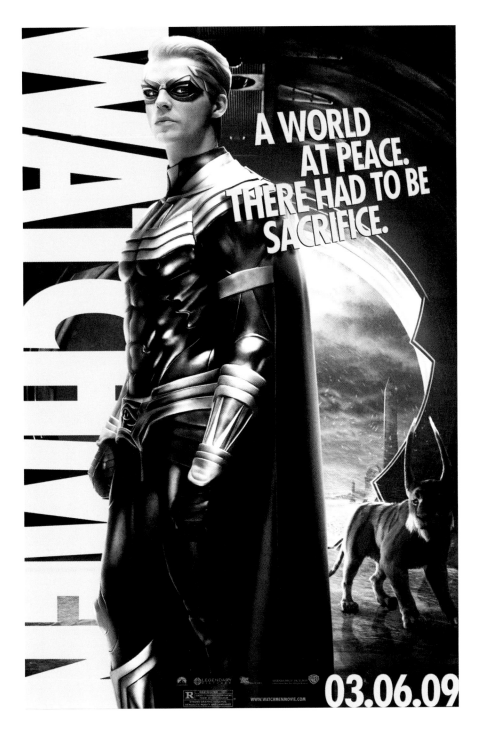

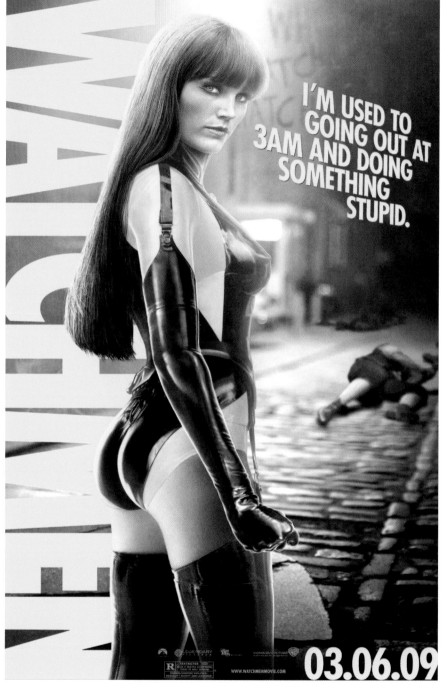

Zack Snyder and the producers of *Watchmen* would like to extend a sincere thank you to all of the incredible artists, designers, photographers, actors, technicians and countless others who through their wealth of talent and tireless dedication helped to bring this film to life. It has been an amazing journey and we are incredibly grateful to have been able to share it with each and everyone of you. In addition, we would like to express our gratitude to everyone at Warner Bros., Paramount Pictures and Legendary Pictures.

Titan Books would like to thank Zack Snyder, Deborah Snyder, Larry Gordon, and Lloyd Levin for their enthusiastic co-operation, and especially Wes Coller, without whom this book would simply not have happened. Our thanks also go to Dave Gibbons for his support, and to the indefatigable John Morgan at DC Comics.

Peter Aperlo would also like to thank Eric Matthies for conducting and transcribing the vast majority of the interviews.

ACKNOWLEDGMENTS